Perhaps this is the first book written surrounding the life of Jether. C.T. Lloyd Spear ties in other Bible characters, lessons from his own childhood, and extended family and friends. This book also recaps experiences and illustrations gleaned from over forty years of public ministry. Those who know the author will recognize his wit and candor. Regardless of your level of spiritual maturity, you will find points of application to your life.

George W. Cheek, C.E.O.
Maranatha Ministries, Maxwell, Nebraska

Present day media is attempting, and succeeding in replacing Bible-based faith as the predominant motivating force in the lives of our young people. The book, *Still A Kid!* by C.T.L. Spear will encourage you in your Christian walk. As you read, you will become part of the moving, down-home stories he shares from his life and the life of others. If I may feature one quote from the book, it would be: "Every failure to act in faith sounds an alarm that should send us back to careful, prayerful meditation on the Word." *Still A Kid!* will inspire, challenge, and motivate one to "stay in the Book," and "stay in the battle!"

Dr. Don Margheim, Professor of Pastoral Studies
Oklahoma Baptist College

Still A Kid! by C.T.L. Spear was a challenge to me. His emphasis on making wise decisions at the right time is so important in life. This book would be helpful for every young Christian and should be required reading for all Bible College students.

Dr. William Hiltz, Academic Dean
Baptist Bible College Canada & Theological Seminary

Fasten your seatbelt! You are about to meet a Biblical character whom you've never met before! He is dressed in warm and homespun cloth by the writer, C.T. Lloyd Spear. The light will shine on a very dimly lit and seldom visited part of God's word. You will be challenged to step up, show up, and grow up! A quick and interesting read for a thirsty heart!!

Dr. William Boyd, Chancellor
College of Biblical Studies, Houston, Texas

In *Still A Kid!* C.T. Spear systematically and thoroughly examines the life of a character that is only mentioned in the Bible a few times. His investigation provides numerous theological and practical challenges that encourage Christians to choose to live their lives in a manner worthy of their calling, regardless of life's circumstances. This book also speaks to non-Christians about the necessity of a relationship with Jesus Christ and its many benefits. Very few books simultaneously speak to both audiences, and do it well.

Dr. Ken Moffett, Assistant Professor of Political Science
Southern Illinois University Edwardsville

Sprinkled with anecdotes of his own childhood and those of the Biblical character, Jether, the author paints a vivid picture in *Still A Kid!* Incredibly, choices that we consider miniscule can change the whole course of life. C.T. uses his past experiences as well as examples from others to illustrate Biblical truths. This book is a much needed reminder to each of us of the need to "go on to maturity in the Lord" lest we, like Jether, should fail in life's conflicts.

Dr. Mickey Johnson, European Field Administrator
Baptist Missions to Forgotten Peoples

STILL A
KID!

*To my dear Bro Floyd
Thanks for your
service,*

Isa 58:12

C.T.L. SPEAR

STILL A KID!

You're young only once, but you can be immature your whole life.

TATE PUBLISHING & *Enterprises*

Still a Kid!
Copyright © 2008 by C.T.L. Spear. All rights reserved.

This title is also available as a Tate Out Loud product. Visit www.tatepublishing.com for more information.

No part of this publication may be reproduced, stored in a retrieval system or transmitted in any way by any means, electronic, mechanical, photocopy, recording or otherwise without the prior permission of the author except as provided by USA copyright law.

All scripture quotations are taken from the Holy Bible, King James Version, Cambridge, 1769. Used by permission. All rights reserved.

This book is designed to provide accurate and authoritative information with regard to the subject matter covered. This information is given with the understanding that neither the author nor Tate Publishing, LLC is engaged in rendering legal, professional advice. Since the details of your situation are fact dependent, you should additionally seek the services of a competent professional.

The opinions expressed by the author are not necessarily those of Tate Publishing, LLC.

Published by Tate Publishing & Enterprises, LLC
127 E. Trade Center Terrace | Mustang, Oklahoma 73064 USA
1.888.361.9473 | www.tatepublishing.com

Tate Publishing is committed to excellence in the publishing industry. The company reflects the philosophy established by the founders, based on Psalm 68:11,
"The Lord gave the word and great was the company of those who published it."

Book design copyright © 2008 by Tate Publishing, LLC. All rights reserved.
Cover design by Joey Garrett
Interior design by Janae J. Glass

Published in the United States of America

ISBN: 978-1-60696-276-3
1. Christian Living: Practical Life: Personal Growth
2. Christian Living: Spiritual Growth: General

08. 10. 24

To Adrian & Juanita House

Whose strategic influence guided
our most crucial decisions.

Whose selfless sacrifice made Christian
hospitality more than a theory.

Whose dedication to Christ remained
steadfast through the severest trials.

Whose humor found entertainment even
in dangers, toils, and snares.

Whose decisive choice to make disciples inspired so many.

ACKNOWLEDGMENT

This book grew from a seed planted by high school Literature teacher, Robert Pospisel, who suggested he saw a glimpse of talent. My double aunt,* Lucile Bashford, confided her own journalistic dreams and urged me to fulfill mine. Dr. Waldo Harder, President of my Alma Mater, ran my first published article in *Grace Tidings*. The discipline of writing monthly copy for *Western Witness* and the *Focus on Western* radio program was an assignment from Adrian House, my pastor, mentor and President of Western Bible College. His confidence catapulted my dreams to new plateaus. Professor William Boyd complimented the writing style of a rookie staffer. It was a kindness never forgotten. The encouragement and criticisms of many residents of Wyoming pushed me to keep writing letters on a variety of topics to the editor of Casper's Star Tribune.

Thank God for some whose loyalty seems to know no bounds, who have promoted and applauded my every attempt: my brother and lifelong pal, Dale, who taught me some of the most significant hidden details of Jether's family, setting this book in motion; enthusiastic promoter and prayer supporter, Lt. Col. Garry R. Rhoades, D.D., Retired, now in Heaven; and best of all, my longsuffering self-sacrificing sweetheart, Sharen, who along with our kids, Dayna, Kendra, and Casey endured enough preaching about Jether to make them suppose he was one of the least obscure of Biblical personalities. They believed in me when I had lost sight of the vision.

*Lucile is the author's maternal and paternal aunt, his father's younger sister who married his mother's twin brother, Lyle Bashford.

TABLE OF CONTENTS

17 · Decisions of Consequence

19 · Life's Pivotal Decisions

35 · Deciding to Develop Faith

59 · Deciding to Depend on the Father

75 · Deciding Determines the Future

87 · Deciding is a Process

97 · Errors of Jether's Fatal Decision

FOREWORD

I had the privilege of knowing the author as a pastor to churches in Wyoming and Colorado. I have observed his effective ministry of evangelism in churches and as a Chaplain in prisons. It is now my delight to be a co-laborer with him in worldwide missions. Most of all, he and his wife, Sharen are dear friends to my wife and me. In his book about Jether, two lessons stand out: One is the importance of making the right decisions. Decisions are the hinges on which our future hangs, so we need to anticipate and be especially careful about our decisions. The other lesson is on the topic of faith. I love Brother Spear's statement, "The development of faith is predicated upon repeated decisions to choose the current test of faith. Faith is never passive. It cannot be stored in batteries. It is active." Readers will greatly be challenged and have their lives strengthened. The Lord is good, all the time.

Dr. Gene Burge, President
Baptist Missions to Forgotten Peoples

DECISIONS OF CONSEQUENCE

Basic Combat Training recruits welcomed graduation day at Ft. Sill, Oklahoma. We attended family day events and arrived early the next day for the commencement exercise. Soldiers received passes to leave the base until 10:00 o'clock p.m., a welcome vacation for the remainder of the day. Since our son was not scheduled to ship out immediately, another pass was anticipated the next day. But, some of the new graduates made foolish decisions that affected the entire battery. One soldier arrived back on base drunk, and another was arrested because some of his guests shoplifted in the PX the afternoon following graduation.

While the entire battery stood at attention with family members present, the Drill Sergeant dressed them down. The drunken soldier would receive an Article Fifteen, have his rank reduced to E-1, and never be permitted promotion above a certain rank. His military career was destroyed by one foolish decision. More than two hundred seventy soldiers were penalized to emphasize the point that one man's decision affects the whole army on the battlefield.

Families who had flown to Oklahoma for the graduation had airline departures that could not be changed. Mothers and sweethearts wept, and men cursed bitterly because they had to go home without a last goodbye to their soldier. The trainees who had obeyed regulations were fighting mad, too.

The metaphor of warfare is one of the most prominent uses of imagery throughout the Bible. From the flaming sword forbidding reentry to the Garden of Eden to the final battles of Revelation, the conflict between God and Satan, good and evil, light and darkness appears on nearly every page and in every genre, whether history, poetry, prophecy, the lives of Christ and the apostles, or in letters to the churches or individuals.

Young Timothy, often characterized as timid, needing encouragement to aggressively pursue ministry responsibilities and lead decisively, was warned to "…endure hardness as a good soldier of Jesus Christ…"[1]

Just as the Bible speaks authoritatively on every subject from history to prophecy, it provides an inexhaustible index of examples, illustrations, and experiences to illuminate the path of life from the cradle to the grave, and is an unparalleled resource for inspiration in every situation we may face. Every day life is filled with heartaches, joys, challenges, discouragement, and new horizons. The snippet that is Jether's biography illustrates how meditation on scripture bolsters us for life's pivotal decisions.

LIFE'S PIVOTAL DECISIONS

"And he said unto Jether his firstborn, Up, and slay them. But the youth drew not his sword: for he feared, because he was yet a youth." Judges 8:20

During one episode of pioneer comedy radio's Amos and Andy Show, Amos asked Kingfish why he had such good judgment. Kingfish replied, "Well, good judgment comes from experience." After several moments of deep reflection, Amos asked tentatively, "Then, where does experience come from?" The wise old Kingfish was ready. "From bad judgment!" he declared.

Samuel Taylor Coleridge, the English Romantic poet who wrote *The Rhyme of the Ancient Mariner* had an unusually gifted son named Hartley. Though family and friends had high hopes for the future of the young man who won an Oriel Fellowship, he lost his Oxford scholarship, wasted his best opportunities, and wandered through life apparently without purpose, drinking without restraint. Years passed. Visiting his parents, Hartley picked up an old textbook from

Oxford. He thumbed through the book, then turned to the flyleaf and wrote these words:

> "Only seventeen years have passed over me since this book was given to me. Then, all looked forward with hope and joy to what I was to become. Now, every mother prays that her lamb; every father hopes that his boy, will never become what I have become." He once described himself as "a thriftless prodigal of smiles and tears."[2]

Opportunity knocks but once. Several decades ago on a Wednesday evening, my pastor announced that he would take a group to Bible camp next summer. As he described what camp would be like, my friends and I glanced at each other with growing enthusiasm. I was a fourth grader. The pastor announced the age requirement for camp was fourth through sixth grade. Wow! My best friends in our fledgling church were both a year older, and I realized that I was barely old enough to go. Then he announced the price: nine dollars for the week, plus a registration fee of fifty cents to be paid soon. My heart sank. I knew it was a lot of money.

A DOLLAR WAS BIG MONEY

My Dad was frequently unemployed in those days, and we lived in a four room house which had railroad ties for a foundation and no plumbing. A dollar was big money to us. At the gas station in those days, before self service and credit cards, my parents would usually say, "Put in a dollar's worth, please."

How amazed and thrilled I was after the service when my mother extracted a fifty-cent piece from her purse and asked if I wanted to go to camp. The rest of the money was earned on odd jobs such as mowing Effie Walker's lawn with her reel-type push mower with no engine or electric motor—just push, push, push to clip those heavy bladed grasses that grow in the Nebraska panhandle.

Finally, the day arrived and we traveled two hundred miles to camp. Our beds assigned, I managed to get the top bunk! After the evening service and a trip to the snack shop, our counselor prayed with us and "lights out" was announced. Excitement was running high in the old barracks style dormitory. Lots of whispering, snickering, and hushing continued for about an hour. A thunderstorm moved in, with flashes of lightning, claps of thunder, and a deluge. It was a real gully-washer. The roof leaked right over my bunk, soaking my bedding and mattress. But I didn't complain. I feared they might send me home. That storm and endless hum-a-zoo tunes complete the memories of my first week at camp. For the next two summers I went to camp for fun and games. But, the direction of my life changed forever because of the spiritual impact of that camp and the pastors who took us there during the next eight years.

One night, I responded at the close of an evening service, surrendering my life to be used by God in any way He planned. Maranatha Bible Camp was the crossroads of opportunity for me. Decisions rooted in my camp experience led me to become the first gospel preacher of record in my family. Motivations nurtured there brought me through college and seminary, as God showed me the unique path designed for me. It all began when I was still a kid!

STILL A KID

Jether is one of those obscure characters of the Bible overlooked by most of us.[3] He is even more obscure than Jabez, whose name appears three times in two verses,[4] and who shares his name with a remote town in Judah where scribes conducted business. Though the name Jether appears eight times in scripture, the young man of our story is mentioned only once by name, and alluded to once again in such a fashion as to escape all but those with a particular interest in his family history.

Some might identify Jether as the firstborn son of one of the most famous of the Judges of Israel. Sunday school children learn the story of Gideon, but few take note of Gideon's children. Their failure to attract our attention and the reason for that failure is the key to the real message of Jether's life.

Gideon and his troop of warriors returned from battle before sunrise.[5] They had taken captive two leading enemies, Zebah and Zalmunna, who had killed Gideon's brothers. When the moment of reckoning arrived, Gideon interrogated them to verify that they were the ones who had killed his brothers at Tabor. When he was convinced of their guilt, he turned to Jether, his son, barking the command, "Up and slay them." But the narrative reports in the hollow, dismal tones of defeat, "But the youth drew not his sword: for he feared, because he was yet a youth."[6]

All we know about Jether's entire life is encapsulated in that short story where his name appears only once. The opportunity of a lifetime was trashed in a moment of indecision; because he was still a kid. With his poor sense of judgment, he probably didn't even realize how significant those few moments actually were. Like many of us, it may have been years before he grasped the weight of that momentous verdict.

TO BE A KID AGAIN

Among my earlier memories is my first day of kindergarten. My parents had moved to Cheyenne, Wyoming, where we lived in a "subdivision." A man had purchased several old railroad boxcars, removed the wheels, and remodeled them into rental housing. Our home was one of those two room boxcars, complete with a path to the tiny outhouse at the rear of the lot.

My mother walked with me to the top of the hill near our home with my little brother clinging to her neck. She leaned down, giving me a hug and kiss, wishing me well as I ventured off to Kindergarten. Rossman Elementary School was visible perhaps two blocks from our humble home, a short walk down the gravel road. I started off valiantly. We had already visited the school, and met my teacher. My class met half days in the afternoon. It was a warm sunny autumn day in Cheyenne.

I doubt that I covered more than ten or fifteen steps before I wheeled around, overcome with emotion, and scurried back to Mama's waiting arms, where I cried while she comforted and encouraged. She reminded me that my cousin Lin was already at school and would not be far away, in the next classroom. I ventured forth again, but lost heart within less than a block, returning for another hug and pep talk. I'm not sure how many refueling trips it took before I finally gained sufficient courage to go all the way to school, looking back frequently to be sure Mama and Dale were still keeping watch over me. I was just a kid.

When I got into the inner circle of the Kindergarten crowd, many recesses were occupied with our favorite game. The older boys were high jumping. I watched them and anticipated the day when I would arrive at the long-awaited goal of being a big kid. But, meanwhile, instead of highjumping and pole vaulting, we played "house." We created those architectural masterpieces by drawing lines in the sand to represent walls. There were frequent spur-of-the moment changes from our original design, and squabbles over who was going to be mom or dad, and who would have to accept the lowly position of "brother" or worse, "little brother or little sister." We were just kids.

There is really nothing wrong with being a kid. Everyone ought to be one for awhile. As I grew older, we moved back to our native family home in the panhandle of Nebraska. There, I graduated from playing "house" to the older students' games at the country school. We played workup, softball, basketball, cops and robbers, cowboys and Indians, and other pastimes of childhood. At home, we rode our bicycles, built a little car using baby carriage axles, rode my cousin's Cushman motor scooter, went fishing, camped out near the river, and built a fort in the gullies of the eroded badlands area on Granddad's farm. It was great! We were kids.

In seventh or eighth grade, I began to envy the kids who went to high school in town. You could get a school permit to drive at fourteen, which seemed far better fun than the activities of elementary school. My parents drove the five and a half miles to and from school at first, and I realized that just being in high school was not really "where it's at!" Actually, one has not truly arrived until he has his own car. After much long agony, my day came. I suppose I'm the only kid in the world who can truthfully say, "My Granddad gave me the Willys!" Yup, it wasn't a Willys Jeep, though. It was a 1952 Willys Aerowing, a two door sedan that was "ugly as a mud fence stake and ridered with tadpoles," as old timers used to say. The first day I drove onto the school parking lot, guys gathered around with more sneers than a stray dog has fleas. Sarcasm dripped as they demanded, "What kinda car is that?" Sometimes being a kid has its downside.

My Dad always said, "I wish I was a kid again, a-doin' what I did again." But, he never explained those longed-for memories. The senior high history teacher told us, "You'd better enjoy high school… life will never be this good again." Fortunately, I hasten to report: he was wrong about that. I got into fights more than once during those years. Both eyes blackened and a broken nose is not my idea of fun. Those immature methods of conflict resolution gradually gave way to better anger management. Sometimes I'm glad I'm not a kid anymore.

Once, a kid named Robert challenged me to a drag race on the highway north of town. He declared his homely old Buick straight eight with a slush pump transmission could mop up my Willys. What an insult! But, he was right. An older wiser me learned to walk away from the duel and avoid humiliation. Kids sometimes lose.

In my Willys, I chased a kid named Joe through streets and alleys of our small town during the lunch hour shortly after receiving my driver's license. Suddenly, the local police cruiser loomed in my rearview mirror. Joe and his passengers got away. Bill Smith, the patrolman whose wife attended our church, invited me to his cruiser where he shamed me as he explained how disappointed he was to think that I would endanger the lives of others so thoughtlessly. I never did it again. Some kids don't get off the hook so easily.

A boy attended our vacation Bible school held during the summer after my sixth grade. He had a reputation for being a tough kid, but our pastor led him to Christ after class one day. He attended Sunday school spasmodically, but never became faithful. To my knowledge, he never evidenced any spiritual growth. Shortly after that, our church started a mission in another town, and my family was part of the new church. I lost track of Bill until five years later, except for rumors about his drinking, fighting and an incident when I heard him mock the pastor who had led him to Christ. His pal drove his mother's high powered car on loose gravel and lost control at ninety miles per hour. Without a seatbelt, my friend crashed through the windshield head first and was airborne some thirty yards, landing on his chin. The impact broke his neck, damaged internal organs, and punctured his lungs. He died at the scene. He was just a kid, but his last decision was fatal. His funeral made some kids think again.

Thirty years ago, Reader's Digest quoted Bill Moyers, "Why use 'you only live once' as an excuse to throw it away?"[7] Throughout history kids have been kids. But sometimes choices we face are "for keeps." You can be a kid only once, but you can be immature all your life!

WHAT LOCKS US INTO IMMATURITY?

Jether was the son of the greatest man of faith of his generation. Gideon is the only man of his era listed in the Bible's Hall of Faith found in Hebrews chapter eleven. The book of Judges spans about four hundred years, so it is unlikely that Gideon lived during the same decades of history as Deborah, Barak, Jephthah, Samson, or Samuel. Yet, even though Jether had a front row seat in many of his father's exploits, he never stepped up to the plate. The scenario is not unusual. Many famous fathers have failed to assist their own sons to the heights of achievement they attained.

A defense of Jether would not be difficult to construct. The big picture reveals that Gideon himself lapsed into idolatry toward the end of his life. He had many wives and at least one concubine.[8] And, Jether, along with his seventy brothers, was killed by an over-ambitious half-brother, Abimelech.[9]

They don't give us all the gory details about Gideon in Sunday school. Usually, they tell about his fleece, his drastically reduced army of three hundred, and the nighttime assault on the Midianites. Unless you take time to make a personal investigation into Gideon's biography, you might suppose he was Superman's great granddad. The facts reveal a man of great weaknesses and many sins. Nonetheless, he took amazing steps of faith and was dramatically blessed in spite of his lapses into pagan religion. On the other hand, a cursory reading of his idolatrous practices might cause us to minimize the sinfulness of the self-centered phases of his life. But it all comes out in the wash: Gideon's family paid the price for his foolish abandonment of Godly living. Jether and his brothers may have supposed that Gideon's exploits of faith were merely powerful positive thinking in shoe leather. If so, they missed the truth. The final sacrifice of Gideon's refusal to continue to walk by faith very likely included his own sons' eternal souls.

But, scripture is clear about individual accountability. Though Gideon failed to influence his children to live the life of faith, and is accountable for that failure, his children too, will give account for their choices. Jether cannot get by with a whining excuse about his dad's idolatry and immorality. All of us, like Jether, will face the opportunities we had, whether wasted or invested. It will never do to excuse ourselves on the basis of being "*just a kid*."

PATIENCE, MY LAD

Sometimes dads scuttle their children into the doldrums of immaturity by their own impatience. Like other impetuous leaders, Gideon was a shoot-from-the-hip kind of guy, and a loner who executed his plans with minimal communication to his followers. Impatient leaders keep followers on their toes and edgy with anxiety. It is difficult to contend with an impatient leader. Impatience produces shell shocked followers, especially in the home. When dad seems impossible to please, children become discouraged and give up. Paul told the Colossian dads, "Fathers, provoke not your children to anger, lest they be discouraged."[10]

My granddad was an entertaining personality, but also a man with heavy burdens, along with apparent disillusionment from unfulfilled dreams. His immediate family often bore the impact of his anger and impatience. I recall many incidents while repairing barbed wire fence, working livestock, or other chores when he lost patience with me. Things were never attempted because we felt disqualified by Granddad's impatient attitude. He was a skillful animal trainer, capable of great patience with a dog or horse. My cousin always seemed to win his approval, but I was more intimidated than encouraged. My brother mirrored Granddad's impatience and rage, but he kept a safe distance, and perhaps never learned to appreciate the more intellectual and reflective facets of Granddad's colorful personality.

My dad was also intimidated by Granddad. I recall incidents in which my dad was livid with anger because he felt his own father's disapproval, even as a grown man. We became men of rage, exhibiting it in various ways. A childhood friend of mine had an indomitable will like Granddad. I bragged about his exploits to my grandfather, saying, "He's just like you, Granddad. And isn't it amazing that his name is George, too?" I remember a pained expression on his countenance. He made no comment. It was probably a wake-up call for him.

As I grew older, I told people that Granddad could have been a Napoleon or Alexander the Great. I now realize that indeed, he did have unusual potential, but was frustrated and angered by the circumstances with which he had to cope. His wife died at age twenty-nine leaving him with two young children and a hospitalization debt exceeding $60,000, the equivalent of a million dollars or more in today's economy. It was 1926, just before the great depression and the dust bowl years that devastated so many homesteaders on undeveloped irrigated land.

Though Granddad could thrill us by the hour, telling of

battles he had won against bullies at school or on the job, I doubt he realized that some of us could never see ourselves measuring up. My dad confided some of his experiences, battles lost and running from bullies. Once, at the old country school, several of the older boys had Daddy down on the playground attempting to pry his mouth open to force-feed a rotten banana peel. Lucile, his little sister—three and a half years younger—who never achieved the stature of five feet, grabbed a baseball bat, and waded in, swinging left and right, clearing the playing field. She adopted or inherited Granddad's unconquerable willpower and has always remained indomitable in relationships.

In high school, Daddy said he was shoved and threatened, challenged to fight, but tried to avoid conflict. In class, a kid taunted him and promised to whip him after school. He said he managed to get to his Dodge touring car and tore out of the parking lot, determined to escape without a fight. But before he reached the intersection, his foe stepped out of the main entry and yelled his name, calling his mother an uncomplimentary epithet. Dad shifted the car into neutral and killed the ignition. Steering toward the curb, he pulled the emergency brake and leaped out of the moving vehicle. Running back to where the challenger stood, he attacked violently in a rage of defense for his mother who had died four years earlier. They fought mercilessly, exchanging blow upon blow as the aggressor backed up step by step. Finally a triumphant blow crashed through, knocking the other teenager to the ground on the cinder parking lot. A janitor pulled my dad off. He had his enemy facing down, straddling his back. Grasping an ear in each fist, he was methodically jamming the kid's face into the cinders over and over again.

Today, he would have been charged and brought to court. I am told the other boy's face was permanently scarred by the cinders. Dad might have gone to prison for mayhem. No charges were filed. In the America of 1930, people believed differences were best settled man to man. Daddy said the other students always gave him a wide berth after that, and I think he was glad he didn't have to keep battling.

Several years later, Daddy's impatience led to a disastrous decision and a hard lesson. Driving a semi truck loaded with grain, he found himself behind another driver on a narrow hilly road. The other driver seemed oblivious of the truck behind him, chuckling along at a snail's pace. Dad tried to pass, but the other vehicle wandered aimlessly over into the passing lane, preventing the pass. After several attempts, patience wore thin, and in a fury Daddy determined he would not be cut off again. He downshifted and floored the throttle, steering into the oncoming lane. The truck was loaded to capacity, so progress was slow, but he kept gaining. Side by side they rolled onto a long narrow bridge spanning a canyon. By now he was in an illegal passing zone, but annoyed with and enraged at the other driver, he determined to get around him. The situation apparently spooked the other driver, who lost control of his vehicle and crashed through the bridge rails into the canyon below. He survived, but never recovered from his injuries and never walked again. A lawsuit, settlement, and a lifetime of regrets followed, making my dad one of the most cautious drivers I've known.

Impatience and road rage exacted an awful price, but divine mercy intervened, limiting the consequences.

SINS OF THE FATHERS

The sins of fathers are visited upon the children. It doesn't have to be so. But the only way to escape that consequence is to love the Lord supremely. God says the sins of fathers are visited upon the children unto the third and fourth generations "of them that hate me."[11] He explains in the next verse that He shows mercy, "unto…them that love me." Sins of wrath, like other sins, can only find release in the mercy of the Heavenly Father who is most patient. Indeed, He is the champion of longsuffering.

I do not pretend that I have mastered the technique. But being aware of it, I am learning to use it. How sad to observe children who are continually victims of their fathers' impatience. Sadness is exponentially multiplied when I meditate upon the effect my impatience has had upon my own children and wife. This is not Granddad's problem. I can't blame my dad for this. I am fully responsible for sowing the seeds of impatience in my own field, perpetuating the anger, rage, impatience, reactions of inferiority and nurturing the comfortable reluctance to act decisively. With regret, I admit that, in some ways, I'm still a kid.

COMFORTABLE IN FAILURE

Jether is not the only kid who felt safe in defeat and failure. It was his comfort zone. He was used to living there in the shadow of his bigger-than-life dad. I wonder if his dad

Still a Kid!

ever realized his own responsibility for the boy's reluctance to take the step of faith.

Champions are made, not born. There is no Super Bowl ring without effort. How do women and men who have all the odds against them manage to succeed? Yet, some who have opportunity laid at their feet never get their engines started! The answer is on display in the museum case of the decision of Jether. Or perhaps, to be accurate we should label it the *indecision* of Jether. Remaining undecided, he could maintain his comfort in the familiar territory of failure.

A professional driver for many years, one of Dad's favorite one-line sermons about the craft of driving was, "Indecision causes wrecks." The motto works for defensive driving, and also for navigating through life. You just can't afford not to decide. Recognize the immaturity of indecisiveness. Grow up! Decide.

DECIDING TO DEVELOP FAITH

"But the youth drew not his sword... the sword of the Spirit, which is the word of God... faith cometh by hearing, and hearing by the word of God." Judges 8:20, Eph. 6:17, Rom. 10:17

Jether's penchant for immature decision was probably ingrained long before the day he faced Zebah and Zalmunna. Though we do not know Jether's age, it appears that he was riding with a platoon or battalion of soldiers, outfitted with the armament of a cavalryman. It is doubtful that he would have been placed in this situation, especially by his war-savvy father, without some level of training. He was expected to be prepared for battle, though he was young, and perhaps, small for his age or baby faced. Zebah and Zalmunna begged to be killed by a seasoned warrior to avoid the disgrace of dying at the hand of a boy.[12]

It may be that Jether did well in training. He may have earned honors in ROTC. Like David's older brothers, Eliab, Abinadab, and Shammah, he appeared to be ready for conflict. But just like those hapless warriors, he lacked the one ingredient for success against the foe: aggressive, confident faith.

Some might protest that the character trait he lacked was courage. Brian Tracy, guru of sales motivation and Psychology of Achievement says, "Courage is the foremost of the sales virtues."[13] Plautus said, "Courage in danger is half the battle."[14] Yonge's Cicero declares, "A man of courage is also full of faith."[15]

FAITH: HOW DO YOU GET IT?

Some imagine that faith is a gift dropped out of Heaven on the spur of the moment. On the contrary, God has granted to every one of us "the measure of faith."[16] But that faith must be increased, developed, and exercised. This is a process: "Faith cometh by hearing and hearing by the word of God."[17] The Psalmist explains that those who are blessed "go from strength to strength,"[18] which seems to parallel Paul's observation that "therein is the righteousness of God revealed from faith to faith."[19] Development of faith is step by step, layer by layer. David's confrontation with Goliath was not mere bravado or reckless abandonment. It was an act of faith: an act which proceeded out of a heart full of confidence in God, based upon repeatedly reviewing, meditating upon, and attempting tests of the promises of God, the object of his faith.

The development of faith is predicated upon repeated decisions to choose the current test of faith. Faith is never passive. It cannot be stored in batteries. It is active. That is why James tells us that faith is seen in works. You can't see the electricity in a flashlight battery, but when the switch is on, anyone can observe that it works.

An attack upon Zebah and Zalmunna would have been

the exhibition of faith that works. But Jether did not initiate an attack because he had failed to develop faith to trust God at the crucial moment. In fact, his mustard-seed sized faith could have won the day, but he never flipped the switch of decision.

ONE BOY WAS STILL A KID

The drama unfolds, "…the youth drew not his sword." Maybe Jether excelled in sword drills in basic training or won the fencing award. But, in the heat of the moment, he could not trust his own ability. Nobody should. We ought to develop our abilities, honing skills to precision. But when conflicts of life close in upon us, faith must be focused on a greater power and ability than our own. The Bible declares, "The sword of the Spirit…is the Word of God,"[20] and "The Word of God is…sharper than any two-edged sword."[21]

David practiced with a slingshot until he could have won a tournament. But, when he faced Goliath, he made no boast of his expertise. He loudly proclaimed, "I come to thee in the name of the Lord of hosts, the God of the armies of Israel."[22] If David had missed his opportunity to kill Goliath, he might have been an unknown Israeli shepherd serenading sheep all his life. The difference between David and Jether was…one of them was still a kid in matters of faith.

Jether didn't do what a soldier should do. Failing to draw his sword, he revealed his lack of confidence in its use. A soldier must master his weapons. The degree of familiarity with the firearm required of modern infantrymen is legendary. He must be able to break it down and reassemble it blindfolded. The sharpshooter or sniper develops such complete latitude with his armament that it is essentially part of his body.

The purpose of the drill is not preparation for parades or color guards, but to incorporate procedures and streamline the dexterity with which they are executed. Only when the weapon is truly mastered, can the soldier give full concentration to enemy movement and anticipate the proper strategy to be employed.

THEY BOTH KNEW

Both David and Jether had to know the inspired quote documented by Joshua, who led Israel into the promise land on a dry path through the Jordan River.

> "This book of the law shall not depart out of thy mouth; but thou shalt meditate therein day and night, that thou mayest observe to do according to all that is written therein: for then thou shalt make thy way prosperous, and then thou shalt have good success." Joshua 1:8

But Jether ignored the fact that it is the Word of God, "quick and powerful, and sharper than any two-edged sword"[23] that makes the difference. David had meditated on the Word as he led his father's sheep, as demonstrated in Psalm 23. Jether was unprepared to draw his sword. His failure in battle revealed his inattention to scripture, which resulted in lack of faith. Maybe it reveals the spiritual vacuum in his childhood home or lack of the kind of mentoring children's and teen workers are called to do. The lifelong impact of Sunday school teachers, children's Bible club leaders, youth pastors, camp counselors, and school teachers has nearly disappeared into oblivion in our media driven culture; but it remains second only to family influence in the development of character and instilling of vision, goals, and passion in the lives of the next generation. Jesus didn't tell us to go into all the world and make students. His command is to make disciples. A student may or may not be motivated to learn. Disciples not only study the material, they imitate the teacher. That is why observers said of Jesus' disciples, "they marveled; and they took knowledge of them, that they had been with Jesus."[24] Jether had been part of Gideon's entourage, but he wasn't like him.

The Spirit of God moves those who are full of the Spirit[25] just like "the Spirit of the Lord began to move" Samson.[26] Job tells us, "There is a spirit in man, and the inspiration (breath, i.e., words) of the Almighty giveth them understanding."[27] When God's Word is breathed into the spirit of a receptive believer, the impulse to act in faith will follow. David meditated upon God's promises and His mighty power. He was compelled to act in faith, because he was as full of faith as the heroes and martyrs of the New Testament era.[28] Every failure to act in faith sounds an alarm that should send us back to careful, prayerful meditation on the Word.

My mother and grandmother supplied me with much material for meditation, including scripture read and memorized, and stories of faith from the Bible, biographies and fiction. Among my earliest memories is that of my mother reading to my brother and me from the tabloid version of the *Young Ambassador* magazine, published by Back to the Bible Broadcast. The fictional hero, Danny Orlis was as real to me as Abraham Lincoln or Noah. I learned to read and devoured more of Bernard Palmer's fiction. I also read fictional stories of Rin Tin Tin, Roy Rogers, Gene Autrey, and others. As a fifth grader, I loaned my copy of Tom Sawyer in exchange for Hopalong Cassidy. My friend was also an avid reader who owned several cowboy books. Before long, I ran out of westerns to trade. I suggested he might like to read Danny Orlis. After reading a few, he asked if I believed in inviting Jesus Christ into my heart as they did in the last chapter or so of every Danny Orlis story. That conversation gave me opportunity to "draw my sword." I led my first convert to Christ during recess after that discussion. Later, his brother came to Jesus, and other family members began attending our church and trusted Christ. At my invitation, over twenty kids from our small rural school attended Real Life Club at our church during my fifth through eighth grades. Several came to Christ, simply because our family was constantly reminded about the life of faith, though I was just a kid.

Think about the kids of the Bible! If Daniel had succumbed to Babylonian prep school policies, he would have failed the quiz of courage and the test of faith. A lowly clerk's position in Nebuchadnezzar's political machine might have been his best opportunity. His memory would be lost today. Indeed, he would never have had to face the prayer crucible... or the lion's den. When abducted from home and taken to a distant land, he was just a kid, but what a kid! What a man!

HE THOUGHT HE MERELY HADN'T DECIDED YET

During my years as a chaplain, I visited a church in a distant community. The pastor introduced me to the congregation as a prison missionary. After the meeting a lady inquired

Still a Kid!

whether I ministered in a certain prison. I replied that most of my work was in that institution. She named one prisoner and asked if I had met him. I had not. She told me of the awful crime for which he had been sentenced, a cruel, merciless murder. With tears, she said, "He's such a fine looking boy. He was in my Sunday school class. I just can't imagine he could ever do such a thing."

Returning to the prison, I watched for him. After several days, he arrived from the processing center. On the yard one day I noticed the name tag on his denim jacket. I introduced myself and told him about the lady who seemed to care a lot about him. After we were acquainted, he stunned me with this remark, "I used to go to church and Sunday school and tried to behave myself. But I *never* listened to anything they said."

He committed the crime as a juvenile and is now serving decades in prison. As a teenager, he thought he merely hadn't decided yet. It turned out that his indecision about developing faith was a crucial decision that impacted his entire life. Now, some might suppose he has plenty of time to decide to develop his faith, but without a major crisis, I suspect he will continue down the path of indecision. The path of least resistance is always the easy choice, inside or outside the prison fence.

Another youthful prisoner said, "Chaplain, I can't be a Christian anymore. I'm going back to being a Buddhist." He expected me to react, but I remained silent. At last I said, "I'm sorry to hear that. But, I want you to know that I'll always be your friend." His real problem was he didn't have enough scriptural understanding of what it meant to be a Christian. He had made a profession of faith in Christ, but only God knows his heart motive. Perhaps he was truly converted, perhaps not. But it was the difficulty of living a Christian life which overwhelmed him.

We sat quietly as seconds ticked by. Then he exclaimed, "I don't know if there are any real Christians in here." He stared at the floor a moment, then faced me and added apologetically, "Oh, I don't mean you, Chaplain…" After another pause, he spoke emphatically, "…and not Bobby either. If there is a real Christian, it's Bobby." Bobby, though incarcerated, had made a watershed decision. Heedless of fear or favor, officer or prisoner, friend or foe, he was determined to trust God and speak out for Christ.

WHAT A CONTRAST

What a contrast I saw between those prisoners. Both were constantly hassled about coming to chapel. But Bobby had survived six years incarceration by daily reading and meditating on the Word of God. Sometimes his use of the Sword was a bit awkward, overconfident, and blustery. Sometimes he'd be discouraged. But he had grown, "precept upon precept…line upon line…here a little, and there a little."[29] The other young man was just a kid, spiritually. But, if he is truly born again, the Spirit of God will continue to speak to him and guide him into tests of faith. A kid can grow.

Maybe it seems your test is too severe. Your companions seem to have an easier path. High tensile steel has to endure more heat, but ultimately, it is far more useful than slag. A.E. Glover and his family walked one thousand miles to get out of China during the Boxer rebellion.[30] They were repeatedly robbed, sick, detained, threatened, starved and jailed.

Other missionaries they knew were simply killed. They often wondered why they managed to get through enemy lines, obtain transportation, food, and clothing. In the end, after they arrived safely across the border, his twenty-eight year old wife gave birth to a sickly baby which soon died. Shortly after, she too died. Why? The Bible answers,

> "Others were tortured, not accepting deliverance; that they might obtain a better resurrection...being destitute, afflicted, tormented; (Of whom the world was not worthy)...God having provided some better thing for us, that they without us should not be made perfect." Hebrews 11:35–40

God has a severely difficult boot camp for the training of his choice warriors. After David faced Goliath, he had to face loneliness, hunger, false accusation, cave dwelling, unsavory companions who once threatened to kill him, a disloyal wife, and a long list of battles and setbacks before he advanced to the throne of Israel. Even as king, he was constantly stretched to trust the Lord in various challenges while leading Israel in conquest, expansion, and administration.

SOME ATTACKS COME FROM WITHIN

Attacks are not always external. The enemy doesn't always loom on the horizon like Goliath, Zebah, or Zalmunna. Some attacks come from within, arising within your home or family, your body or your mind. My friends Jeff and Kelly Franklin have sustained repeated physical attacks. Jeff was diagnosed at Vanderbilt with the fastest form of cancer and told there is no hope for treatment. This happened at least three times, but Jeff confidently asserted he is certain God is not finished with him yet. Kelly was born with Cerebral Palsy and has never walked without crutches. With the help of her well trained teenage daughters, she maintains an immaculate home and served as a pastor's wife. Many would fall apart emotionally if we had to face a single day like Jeff's and Kelly's average day.

Those who struggle with addictions must learn how crucial a single decision can be. Many sexual addicts, now incarcerated, relive the moments of fatal decisions again and again. Druggies and alcoholics must face the importance of a single decision and the factors that influence it if they are ever to maintain sobriety. I quickly lost track of the number of times a prisoner said to me, "Chaplain, I know I would never have done it if I hadn't been drunk." Thousands are serving life sentences for deeds committed in a moment while under an addictive influence.

NOTHING IS IMPOSSIBLE

Years ago, I met Eugene Clark at Maranatha Bible Camp in Nebraska. He weighed about eighty pounds and was blind. His rheumatoid arthritic condition left him in a fetal position confined to a hospital bed in a mobile home on the campground. When I visited him there, he immediately told me a joke about someone he called "crippled." He asked me to entertain him with some of my memorized ditties. There was no hint of discouragement or self pity in his demeanor. I looked around the sparsely furnished room. Taped to the rail of his bed was a dictation unit which he operated, though with some difficulty. I realized that this was his music composition studio.

For several decades before his illness, he was Chairman of the department of music at Back to the Bible Broadcast. He had written and arranged music, edited and published sheet music, songbooks and various materials. He was honored as Alumnus of the Year by Moody Bible Institute. In youth, he was a child prodigy, serving as organist for an influential church before entering his teenage years.

Staring at the dictation machine, I imagined him dictating words and music of original compositions which his wife then played at the nearby spinet piano while he corrected and edited both lyrics and music by ear from his bed. He wrote the music and words of the widely popular choral song, "Nothing is impossible when you put your trust in God…"[31] What a test! What suffering! What triumphant victory! Blind and severely disfigured, in this life his hands would never again play the instruments he loved, but he was still drawing his sword, still maiming the enemy, attacking by faith. It was a demonstration of the role of decision in a mature believer. He was not a kid. His maturity in faith outstrips that of most preachers and theologians or even the martyrs, in all of history.

GOD DOESN'T FORCE MATURITY

God doesn't force his children to mature. Demas can forsake Paul and quit assisting the missionaries. John Mark can bail out and go home to Mama, missing the unique advantage of a front row seat from which to witness God's blessing upon the abundantly fruitful church planting work of Paul. Peter can stand in the outer court of Pilate's judgment hall, because he doesn't understand why Jesus won't let him decapitate his cousin Malchus in the battle of Gethsemane. Other disciples can follow afar off. King Saul can wallow in self pity and seethe with jealous envy. Noah can just get drunk! Samson can take another trip to see the heathen girls of Timnath or Gaza. David can licentiously watch the neighbor's wife instead of deciding to go to battle. They all insist that they didn't intend to decide to do wrong. They were just temporarily undecided.

INDECISION IS NEVER A MOUNTAINTOP EXPERIENCE

"Multitudes, multitudes in the valley of decision..." exclaimed the prophet Joel.[32] Deciding is often pressed upon us in the valley, a place that lacks a clear view of the future. In his textbook, *Principles of Management,* George R. Terry observes, "In many respects, crisis decisions test the true measure of a manager's ability."[33] A good leader knows that "the worst decision is to decide not to decide."[34] Failure to decide opens the floodgate to a deluge of problems which might have been surmounted simply by making a decision and laboring diligently to make the decision work. Delay and deliberation nearly lost the war for Lincoln's Union Army. Those too afraid to decide ultimately cost more and waste more than decisive leaders who inevitably make some bad decisions.

As a young family, we traveled from church to church in a van, pulling a travel trailer. Long hours of traveling and home schooling were sometimes endured more than enjoyed. Somewhere in South Dakota, we stopped at a vacant playground to take a break and let the girls play. Dayna is five and one-half years older than Kendra, so she managed to win the race to the slide and climbed quickly to the platform. The little one tagged along, panting laboriously to the top. Although Dayna arrived first, she stood transfixed in fear as she surveyed the distance and descent of the slide. She couldn't decide. Sharen and I heard her crying and hurried to see if she was hurt. Her only pain was the trauma of indecision. While she agonized over the decision, Kendra slid screaming in ecstasy down the slide, landed on her bottom, banging her head on the slide. No tears. She jumped up, ran around to the ladder, climbed to the top and slid down again, while her sister mourned the anguish of decision.

Though I offer no statistical proof, I think birth order frequently victimizes the firstborn when it comes to decision making. Parents, too uncertain themselves, convey fearful attitudes to the child they overprotect. My own childhood and adolescence were characterized by that same apprehensive indecision. Though I made major life decisions at a fairly early age with apparent confidence, my tendency was to limit myself to arenas in which I felt especially prepared, studiously avoiding the unknown. I have observed many firstborn whose childhood and youth reflect the same pattern. The Biblical writer carefully points out that Jether was firstborn.

PRAYER IS NO SUBSTITUTE FOR DECISION

Jether's reluctance is evidence of a transfer of his dad's vacillation. The most widely known story of Gideon's life is his prayer to God for a sign by dew on a fleece of wool. God had already given clear direction to him, but rather than acting decisively, he prayed for a sign. After God sent the sign,

Gideon prayed again asking for another sign. This time, dew was to be on the ground and the fleece dry. God graciously accommodated Gideon's prayers, but we must wonder if this event merely unmasks the agony of indecision rather than a formula for finding God's direction.[35]

Military leadership, like excellent athletic coaching, is decisive. From the enlisted man to the General, it is the ability to decide resolutely that is respected. Wars and athletic championships are won by decision makers. Nobody does it right every time. When we find ourselves seized with fits of arrogance, thinking we are invincible, or with spasms of inferiority or a loser mentality, we may have to relearn that "pride goeth before...a fall."[36] Indeed, both extremes—arrogance and inferiority—are evidence of self absorption.

Even psychological counseling technique demonstrates that counselors can render significant assistance by merely encouraging the client to decide. Popular media psychologists like Dr. Laura and Dr. Phil frequently pressure their callers or guests into verbalizing a decision on the air or before a live audience. They really do the client a favor by forcing a decision, if they stick to it.

The mentally ill are a vast herd of humanity milling about like cattle in an unfamiliar corral of indecision. The rest of us who think ourselves mentally healthy should consider that our psychological health might be best measured by our responses to decisions. At each end of the spectrum are those whose insanity is evidenced by over-decisiveness—a compulsion to control others, and indecisiveness—unwillingness to take the risk and accept the responsibility for a choice. Most of us are somewhere in between, have been or will be hung up in one of the end zones, out of bounds. Take note. Do your own psychological assessment.

Mack Douglas quotes practicing psychologist, Randall B. Hamrack, "In twenty years, I've talked with, tested and given vocational counsel to at least 10,000 young men and women. One characteristic that almost all had was the tendency to sell themselves short."[37] This may be the underlying reason the new category of counseling labeled Life Coaching has received wide acceptance. We all need coaches in the game of life.

DECIDING ISN'T EVERYTHING

Lest this showcase of decisiveness become a shrine, it should be noted that being a decision-maker is not sufficient of itself to win the real battles of life. David, the warrior, military strategist, and unequalled king of Israel, was decisiveness personified. But, one shoot-from-the-hip choice led to the greatest heartache of his life. As he strolled on the roof of his palace, basking in the accoutrements of the penthouse lifestyle, he saw Bathsheba. He decisively ordered a servant to bring her to the palace. That brief adulterous interlude spawned murder, incest, rebellion, and the spiritual weakening of the nation and his family. He almost lost the kingdom over it.

But, though his cover-up seemed successful and pride led him to stack one sin on another, David's decisiveness won the day again when Nathan preached his famous sermon, "Thou Art the Man!"[38] The king's decision to repent and pay the price of restitution was just as firm and final as his decision to sin. Psalm 51 is the journal of David's repentance. Many Israelites, including General Joab, remained scornful and suspicious of David's spirituality, but history bears witness that his repentance was genuine.

Decision was the key. David could have spent the rest of his life in regret and self-chastisement. He could have focused on penance, as many do, evermore trying to make up for the past. But he recognized the only sacrifice God wants from a believer who sins is "a broken and contrite heart."[39] Perhaps the ministry God gave David through his pen, writing many Psalms and leading his people in sincere worship of his merciful gracious God, was of greater eternal impact than all the military victories and other achievements of his life.

Decision linked to faith in a promise-keeping God who everlastingly loves sinners made the difference, just as it did when he decisively ran toward Goliath with sling in hand. As always, the promises of the Word mixed with faith supercharge the decision with eternal impact.

THE PROBLEM OF WEAK FAITH

Jether "drew not his sword" because his faith was weak. Weak faith is indecisive faith. Strong faith decides and leaves the rest to God. Weak faith is the product of many decisions to delay decision. No choice is a choice. It is almost never a good choice.

Perhaps there is a hidden lesson in Jether's name. It means abundance, excess, superiority, excellence, or overhanging.[40] His resources were abundant. He enjoyed an excess of possessions, feeling superior to others because of his father's wealth and fame. It may be that he enjoyed too much delectable food and was overweight. His upbringing may have focused on excellence to the extreme of perfectionism, making him reluctant to attack for fear of doing it imperfectly. Or he may have been painfully aware that he had used his connections to the captain to avoid the rigors of training designed to prepare him for the challenge. It seems likely that he was spoiled and slothful.

What an apt description of the spiritual condition of many believers today. Like Laodicea, we are rich, increased in goods, and imagine we have need of nothing.[41] On the contrary, we are unprepared, overfed, lazy, and basking in abundance and excess which we suppose justifies our attitude of superiority. In our fixation for excellence, we have become perfectionists who refuse to lift a finger unless we can do it with class. And, like Jether, many are missing the greatest opportunities of life.

WEAKNESS MANIFESTS IN EXTREMES

Observing many churches, I see few believers who will decide. Few church congregations actually choose. Lack of decisive faith is reflected in skimpy giving to missions. Failure to wield the sword of the Spirit in our porn addicted, drug and alcohol infested communities belies our weak faith. We need the thundering ultimatum of Captain Joshua, "Choose you this day whom ye will serve..."[42]

Weak faith often morphs into demanding slave-driving taskmasters of the ministry, who use the Word deceitfully, preaching "outlines" and preferences rather than transferring scriptural precepts line upon line. The Sword is not merely a weapon to be wielded according to the whims of the soldier. It is the Sword *of the Spirit*, guided skillfully by the Holy Spirit. The self aggrandizing success-oriented Christian leader who is climbing destiny's ladder with a self-improvement plan is not focused on faithfulness to the Spirit. He may be decisive, but his decisions are not Spirit led. In Matthew 23, Jesus warned his disciples that the Pharisees were focused on external observances, self promotion, making demands of others, taking advantage of widows, pretending godliness, and exacting tithes, but omitting "the weightier matters of the law, judgment, mercy and faith..." Notice that faith was among Jesus' top priorities.

Jerry,[1] a teenager of my acquaintance, enjoyed an unusual abundance of things money will buy. Though his parents were leaders in their church and highly respected in the community, both were indecisive about discipline issues with their children. The boy was shielded from much of the world outside his home and church, but as a student eager to be popular, he began to drift toward spiritual disaster.

An older teen in the church youth group, Brad, flaunted his bad attitude, mocked the pastor, dropped out of school, and began a lifestyle of drinking, fighting, and illicit sexual encounters. Because of his natural leadership ability, many of the youth were adversely affected, and Church youth attendance dropped to new lows as weaker Christians followed his example. The younger lad bragged to his friends, "I'm going to be just like Brad." Years later, the older boy repented of his sin and gradually earned the respect and admiration of the church and community, but the younger fellow, spoiled, and excused from responsibility, never found the courage to turn away from his sin of choice. He is still dominated by the alcohol that won his acceptance into the elite crowd. The spiritual opportunities of his life, like Jether's, have evaporated one by one.

ARE YOU A JETHER?

Consistent practice with the Sword of the Spirit builds convictions in one who considers the principles of the Word. Hebrews tells us it makes the difference in our level of maturity.

> "when...ye ought to be teachers (mature), ye have need that one teach you again...the first principles...and...have need of milk, and not of strong meat...strong meat belongeth to them that are of full age...who by...use have their senses exercised (developed) to discern both good and evil." Hebrews 5:12–14

The Bible imparts a philosophy of life that guarantees growth toward maturity for those who are Spirit led, walking by faith. The imparting of guiding principles is a process. Isaiah described it. "For precept must be upon precept, precept upon precept; line upon line, line upon line; here a little, and there a little."[43] Spiritual growth involves learning by repetition the truth that affects one's way of life.

During my formative years, my mother or father read the designated scripture and the reading for the day from *Our Daily Bread*, a devotional guide published by Radio Bible Class. This reading was followed by prayer. At the home of my maternal grandparents, my earliest memories are of the daily reading of *The Upper Room* devotional and accompanying scripture. They each prayed. Then, with heads bowed, they quoted,

> "Let the words of my mouth and the meditation of my heart be acceptable in thy sight, O Lord, my strength and my redeemer...and the Lord watch between me and thee when we are absent one from the other."
> Psalm 19:14, Genesis 31:49

I reached adulthood before I realized those were scripture verses. I memorized them before I could read by hearing them so often at my grandparents' table. When we visited my cousin, after breakfast, my aunt read the Bible and *The Upper Room*, published by the Methodists. I just couldn't avoid it. When I ate breakfast, I was sure to be listening to the Bible. "Faith cometh by hearing..."[44]

Using the Sword of the Spirit will build the conviction that God is greater than my problem. David believed that! Jether played hooky the day that concept was taught. Maybe his father failed to incorporate a devotional pattern into family life. After all, Jether's grandfather, Gideon's father, was an idolator. Destroying the family idol was Gideon's first act of faith.[45] I have observed that many first generation believers fail to effectively influence their own home for the long range. Unfortunately, Gideon himself drifted back into idolatry after winning major battles and achieving national prominence. Sometimes spiritual leaders relax from the disciplines that brought victory when they have achieved some level of accomplishment, oblivious to the greater things God has in reserve if they would continue to act decisively in faith.

THE SWORD INSTILLS CONVICTIONS

The Biblical sword builds the conviction that tithing makes sense. God ought to be first![46] Many believers imagine church leaders have ulterior motives in reiterating principles of giving. This is because they have simply espoused the world's money concepts. They fear they will shortchange themselves if they give. These and other truths are spiritually discerned precept upon precept. Each individual must receive it personally. Many continue to chafe against these scriptural concepts because they neglect the proper use of the Sword.

Faithful church attendance helps bring balance. The Word of God demonstrates that association with other believers, learning Bible convictions, and seeing these lived out in others offsets the influence of the world. Many seem never to get it! The Sword is dusty or even rusty in their homes and even in the churches. Though children and teens hear Christian leaders preaching scriptural convictions, their meditation on those concepts is short-circuited by the observation—overt or subliminal—that their own parents must not really attach significant value to these issues. More energy is expended on decisions about which movie to watch, where to go on vacation, or why money was spent for some item than is ever devoted to serious discussion of Biblical lifestyle questions.

Satan manages to pit one parent against the other on spiritual issues such as hospitality, church attendance, giving, involvement in ministries, and cultural issues. This leads to hostility and conflict or silent avoidance, ultimately robbing the next generation of the carefully reasoned, studied opinions and scriptural convictions of their forebears.

Christian service builds a faithful record that brings eternal reward. The Bible teaches that my service for Christ is more important than earthly achievements. This world focuses upon the temporary. But faithful service in small things, such as a cup of cold water given in Jesus' name, will be rewarded in heaven. This conviction, too, is developed bit by bit in those who use the Sword, making the true servant of God patient and kind, gentle as an infant's mother. They realize that character is more vital than accomplishments enshrined in possessions, certificates, trophies, diplomas, and vacations.

UNIQUE METHODS OF SERVICE

Birl Lynch lived a rough life, but was a hard worker in the oil fields of the western states. His parents' poverty made him determined to strike out on his own at age fourteen, leaving them one less mouth to feed. Later, Birl married Eunice, a fifteen year old girl who also knew how to work long productive hours. Their years of labor paid off. They became quite prosperous, owning several companies. When we met, they were dedicated, loyal servants of Christ, but painfully aware of the early years of godlessness and consequent lack of spiritual training and experience. Birl owned a stainless steel Delorian sports car with gull-wing doors. He used it to win the heart of Steve, a boy who rode our bus to Sunday school. Steve will never forget the thrill of riding in that unique car, waving to his neighborhood friends in one of the poorer parts of town. The Lord never runs out of unique methods of service, fitted to the willing believer.

Another couple, Mike and Pam Doyle, lived on the limited income of a Christian school principal, but felt God wanted them to offer Steve a home. His mother recognized that Steve would thrive in such an environment, and allowed him to move in with the Doyle's. Only eternity will reveal how significant was the role of those families in the life of a boy who once rode a bus to church.

Perhaps Jether was born too soon? He never heard a sermon on Ecclesiastes 9:10: "Whatsoever thy hand findeth to do, do it with thy might…" Solomon, divinely inspired,

Still a Kid!

penned those words many years after Jether's lifetime. But, what is in *your* hand? Is it a well worn Bible, often refreshing your mind? Are you growing in grace? Or are you still too immature to decide to make your sword available to your Captain's command?

DECIDING TO DEPEND ON THE FATHER

"And he [Gideon] said unto Jether his firstborn, Up, and slay them." Judges 8:20

Consider this: Is it likely that Gideon would have recklessly jeopardized his firstborn son's life? The scene was set up for Jether to win a victory that had little risk of failure. He was surrounded and backed by the best of his father's army, probably Dad's personal bodyguard. These were tested warriors, who had just returned from a victorious conquest. They were winners. No doubt, Gideon deeply felt Jether's need to face and triumph over a real foe. Like any father, he longed for young Jether to excel. The momentum of recent victory seemed like perfect timing for Jether's debut. Gideon envisioned the welcome home Jether would enjoy and the confidence he would gain racking up a major win. He anticipated the impact this event would have establishing his son's reputation in enemy territory.

But, no matter how masterfully others may rig our success, each individual must make right choices in the heat of battle to attain that purpose. Some have enjoyed apparent success, but because it was purchased by another, they were unable to maintain their status of achievement.

Our Heavenly Father has actually set the stage for your success! However, real success requires your active participation by faith. Will you take advantage of the unique opportunity God has engineered for you?

RECKLESS DECISIONS NOT RECOMMENDED

Jether was handicapped by reluctance to decide, but others plunge in recklessly without considering the potential for disaster in hasty ill-advised decisions. Timing and synergy are crucial. During my tenure as leader of an organization, our landlord refused to extend our lease contract at a reasonable price, insisting the facility was slated for a major demolition and renovation. Instead, he offered another place nearby at a comparable price. Some of our key leadership favored that choice. In view of the necessity of a move, other leaders wanted to make a major relocation to another property. I favored the second alternative. When put to a vote, the other leaders were divided fifty/fifty.

In a reckless moment, I voiced my opinion citing the fact that three who favored the first facility had already announced plans to move or transfer, which meant they would not be there for the moving process or its consequences. I exercised my vote, which swung the decision. Nobody opposed it, realizing the truth of my observation about the departure of the other key leaders. But, in the following months, I found myself virtually without support in the actual process of relocation. After several months of late night prayers, walking alone with God, I realized that the real problem was that I had failed to depend on the Heavenly Father in the decision process. Foolishly, I imagined my years of experience and leadership would carry the weight to assure success in the transition.

Years have passed and I have often wished for an instant replay. If I could relive that scene, I hope I would have wisdom to call upon all the leaders to join me in a period of special prayer, asking God for direction. My viewpoint now is that God was giving us a clear signal in the split vote. It was a signal to halt and seek His leading. Instead, unfortunately, I plunged recklessly onward, imagining that raw decisive leadership alone could save the day.

TIME TO PRAY AFTER DEFEAT

A similar crisis was the experience of the Israelites after their amazing victory at Jericho. Intoxicated with the pride of achievement, they decided to send a small contingent of three thousand soldiers to attack the village of Ai, leaving most of their troops behind. The battle was engaged without prayer. They were soundly defeated, losing thirty-six lives. After the battle, Joshua and the elders found time to pray earnestly. God revealed the root problem of Achan's sin during that prayer meeting.[47] Little do we realize how the sin of one person can poison so many.

At one point I was convinced that we should change the name of our church. Our name, Riverview, was difficult to pronounce. I had noticed that key staff members answered the telephone in haste, not pronouncing distinctly. The result was "Rearview." As I became acquainted in the community, I learned of incidents in which our name had been besmirched by actions of students of our church sponsored school. As an item of business, I presented a name change for consideration to our key leaders. One of the men reacted with a sharp denunciation of the idea. Thankfully, I had presence of mind to table the discussion.

Several months passed. I had committed the matter to prayer and decided it wasn't worth a conflict. One day the same man asked, "When are we going to change the name of the church?" I was astounded that by leaving it in the Lord's hand, our strongest opposition became an enthusiastic proponent of the idea he had first rejected. I came to understand that the fellow only needed time to think through the concept and adopt it as his own.

PARENTS OR MENTORS CANNOT GUARANTEE SUCCESS

A young man inherited a large ranch in the west. His parents worked hard to hand him the fruit of their labors. He scorned their work ethic and sold the ranch as soon as he took possession. He bought a fleet of trucks and went into the transportation business. Before long, mismanagement and inattention to critical details brought him to bankruptcy. At last report, he was renting his former ranch from the new owner, doing the kind of work he despised. Though his parents tried to insure his success, in the end the choices were his own. Like the prodigal son who thought his plan better than his father's, he wound up slurping hog slop, because he refused to make the decision to depend on his father's wisdom. Even Rehoboam, the son of wise Solomon, who inherited the most powerful and wealthy world empire,[48] learned the hard way that parents and mentors cannot guarantee success. Despite the counsel of the most seasoned leaders of his time, he chose a path that caused tragic loss for himself and his country, when more than two-thirds of the tribes seceded from his kingdom.[49]

THE RICH ARE NOT THE ONLY ONES SPOILED

No doubt, Jether felt inferior to his famous dad. But, if his dad had been unknown or less respected, he might have used that for an excuse to delay decision. "The sluggard is wiser in his own conceit than seven men that can render a reason."[50] If you're looking for an excuse, one is as good as another, and possibilities are limitless. There is nothing to be gained by arguing with one who is determined to excuse his faults.[51] Any pastor of brief experience can testify that those who are obsessed with justifying their actions are virtually impervious to even the strongest rebuke. Inferiority feelings often motivate us to construct defense mechanisms built on pride. Yet the pride that exhibits itself in inferiority will rarely admit it is proud.

If Jether felt inferior, it was because he didn't meditate upon the ways of God. He missed the point that God is no respecter of persons. If he had only considered the book of Genesis, which was certainly available to him, he could have recognized the gracious dealings of God with unworthy men such as lying Abraham and cheating Jacob, not to mention Levi and Simeon, the vengeful murderous sons of Jacob who, after repentance, became leading patriarchs of Israel.

THE ENEMY FORGETS OUR SONSHIP

Jether should have known that he could depend on his companions to save his neck. Certainly, his father would have risked his own life to deliver him. But Jether didn't decide to trust. Amazingly, the entire incident seems to have come about because Zebah and Zalmunna failed to recognize the relationship—the sonship—of Gideon's brothers. When Gideon demanded a description of the men they had killed at Tabor, they replied that they looked like Gideon. They "resembled the children of a king."[52] This statement should have gotten Jether's attention. He should have realized how fortunate he was to be the son of such a royal individual as Gideon. His sonship was of paramount importance. If he had merely paid attention to the conversation, it would have provided fuel for his weak faith. How exciting to be the son of the regal Gideon!

The New Testament focuses on sonship. As he introduces Jesus in chapter one of his gospel, John presents Him as the Eternal Word of God, the Creator. Referring to the created ones, especially the Israelites, he notes that this Eternal Word "came unto his own, and his own received him not. But as many as received him, to them gave he power to become the sons of God, even to them that believe on his name:"[53] John's message to all mankind was that those who receive Jesus and believe on his name are given authority (power) to become sons of God.

WHO IS YOUR FATHER, REALLY?

In contrast, Jesus contested the religious leaders' right to call themselves sons of God. In a resounding rebuke, he told them, "Ye are of your father the devil."[54] Contrary to popular opinion, not all sons of Adam or Abraham are sons of God, according to Jesus. John made it clear that only by personally receiving and believing in Jesus the Messiah could any of us classify ourselves as sons of God.

Are you aware of your sonship? What if you were preoccupied with the thought of whose child you are? The realization of your intimate relationship to the most powerful Father in the Universe is certainly worthy of consideration. Have you failed to make the connection...to connect the dots? Jether did.

If you have made the connection, have you contemplated its value? While others quaked in fear at the mere mention of Gideon's name, Jether missed the impact of who his father was. So "while he lingered"[55] like Lot, preoccupied with trifles, the opportunity for which he was born slipped away unnoticed.

REMEMBER WHO YOU ARE

Harry S. Truman, former president of the United States, said, "Remember who you are. Remember where you came from. Remember where you're going."[56] Truman was asked what we can do to combat juvenile delinquency. With typical humor, the president replied, "Pick out their grandparents." Gesturing toward pictures of his own grandfathers on the wall, he related what his pioneer forebears meant to him. "I could not be untrue to my parents and grandparents, to my family tradition," he said. Only his attention to and meditation upon his heritage could have brought to mind such a response. As unthinkable as it was to Truman to be disloyal to his tradition, the contrast is so frequently demonstrated in lives of those of distinctive birth as to make Truman's remark truly remarkable.

Benedict Arnold, whose family established a respected name in the American colonies, became a traitor of such notoriety that his name is synonymous with treason. Judas too, is legendary for his disloyalty to the Lord. Christians bear a name which is above every name. How dare we fail to be loyal to Christ, who paid our sin-debt with his own blood?

While I was a high school student, an older friend graduated and went to Bible College. In a few months he returned home. I admired his steps of faith, so I asked about his plans to return to college. He told me he had learned that the only way to go to Bible College is with a wife and a good car. He said he would go back to school when he had enough money to buy a new car, new clothes, and get married. Months rolled by. He began to seriously date a fine young lady. Shortly, they were engaged. I overheard conversations in which people expressed surprise that the two would make a match. Though inexperienced, I too felt they were mismatched personalities. But, soon they were married and off to college in their new car, packed with new clothes. Tragically, the marriage lasted only a year or two. Since both were my friends, I was sincerely grieved for them. But as I thought about the scenario, I remembered that his explanation about going back to school only when he could afford marriage, a car, and clothes had made me very uneasy. I now believe the Holy Spirit was warning me against his advice. I suspect his statement revealed lack of faith in a Heavenly Father, who provides for his own.

MILITARY CONDITIONING TO OBEY

One of the goals of military conditioning is that of securing absolute obedience from each soldier. Insubordination is tantamount to murder of one's own troops in battle. We must learn to obey immediately and without question when the commander gives an order. Christ has issued many standing orders. Do you obey on impulse? Moody said, "When a man is filled with the Spirit, he can act on impulse and do the will of God."[57] Jether was not moved by such impulses.

YOU ARE UNDER AUTHORITY

God has placed each of us into an authority structure. We are under authority of our government, of a church where God has called us to grow and serve, of a family, and in our employment. Part of living by faith is learning to trust God to use the authority to guide us.

When I was a boy in about fifth or sixth grade, my dad and I visited a man from our church. I don't recall the purpose of our visit, but I remember well the tone of the man's remarks to my father. My parents had known him for many years, and they had survived some difficult experiences together. Years later, I asked my dad about the conversation. He explained that the man had always seemed to gravitate toward and associate with those who were critical of a pastor. This had been true with at least three pastors. As life rolled on, I attended the funerals of both my dad and his friend. The pastors he criticized have all passed on too. But the influence of his attitude toward spiritual leaders left his children to struggle against the Lord's authority in their own lives.

The Holy Spirit indwells each believer to guide us into all truth. He alone can overrule the authority that God has placed over us. It was on this basis that the apostles said, "We ought to obey God rather than men."[58] But, we must depend on those placed around us unless clearly led otherwise by God Himself. Jether was under the authority of a powerful father who was the dynamic fearless leader of the most strategic nation on earth. But the power of authority—his father's, his employer's, his military commander's and spiritual leader's—all fell short of motivating him to decide. What immaturity! What lack of training. What proof that he was still a kid.

FAULTY RELATIONSHIPS TO THOSE IN AUTHORITY

The tragedy for Jether is that his faulty relationship to authority short-circuited the power that would have catapulted him to an overwhelming victory and a significant opportunity in history. Evangelist George Whitefield was a young man from a home environment significantly deficient in spiritual nurture. However, his own decision to immerse himself in scripture and spiritual disciplines apparently transformed him from an unknown inferior fellow student to a trail blazer who pioneered a path for John and Charles Wesley and hundreds of other leaders. His biographer tells us that on his knees he read his New Testament in Greek and English with Matthew Henry's commentary every day for many months.[59] The transformation of young Whitefield was so dynamic that his ministry profoundly affected the British Isles and the new world, impressing even Benjamin Franklin,[60] though Franklin was a self-proclaimed skeptic of religion.

GETTING RID OF FEARS THAT STYMIE DECISION

The heartbreak of Jether's story is that he didn't depend on his own father. But then, do you depend on your father… your

Heavenly Father? Honesty compels us to admit that fears often short-circuit trust. Judges 8:20 tells us that Jether "feared." That is the Bible's explanation for his failure to trust his father. John the Apostle tells us that mature (perfect) love casts out fear.[61] He then explains that fear has "torment." This torment is the harassment of guilt. After Adam sinned, he hid from God. Asked why he was hiding, he explained, "I was afraid."[62] His fear was the product of guilt. Guilt will terrorize you if you go on handling it without Christ's promised intervention. As long as you submit to the tyranny of sin's guilt, you cannot overcome fear. Forgiveness, John tells us,[63] is readily available, removing guilt.

Jesus' words to his own were, "Fear not, little flock."[64] "I will never leave thee, nor forsake thee, so that we may boldly say, The Lord is my helper, and I will not fear..."[65] The good news is that all the guilt of our sin, past, present, and future, has already been punished. The punishment is finished. Jesus Christ has paid the price with his own blood. "As many as received him, to them gave he power (authority) to become the sons of God."[66] If you've received him by faith, believing in your heart,[67] then you are a child of God. He is your Father. Trust your Father! He will not let you down.

WHY WE FAIL TO OBEY

When fear has control, it is because love has not matured to perfection. If Jether had loved his father maturely, as Jesus loved his Father, or as Isaac loved his father, he would have risked his own life to obey. We fail to obey our Father because our love is immature. Its character is more selfish than selfless. Isaac trusted Abraham. He totally depended upon his father's love, placing himself upon the altar to be sacrificed to God.[68] Such calm, mature obedience from a boy! The real issue is not age. It is maturity. Those guilty of cutting corners in the life of faith cannot help being harassed by feelings of guilt which then undercut their commitment to depend on God, though that commitment be sincerely declared, and often repeated. There are no artificial substitutes or shortcuts to maturity.

How can love mature in me? John says, "Whoso keepeth his word, in him verily is the love of God perfected."[69] The love of God is matured in me as I am guarded by his Word. The word "keepeth" is an old English word used in the sense of a sentry who *keep*s the city. He guards the city. It means to be garrisoned by or protected by the Word of God.[70] God's Word is my arsenal of weapons to use against the enemy. When the Word is stacked into my mind like shells, grenades, and bombs in an arsenal, then my love will become confidently mature, able to engage any enemy challenge. My focus can shift from the painful awareness of my inadequacy to strong confidence in the munitions I possess, supplied by my Father. That's the maturity Jether lacked.

FEAR OF THE UNKNOWN

As a seventeen-year-old lad, I left the Nebraska panhandle on the Wyoming border to attend Bible College in Omaha, 500 miles from home. My pastor, Adrian House, a transplant from North Carolina, described it best: "My knees were knockin' *Home Sweet Home* and *Yankee Doodle* at the same time." You might say I was "scairt!" The big city, bus lines, honking horns, streetlights, and multitudes of strangers made me wonder if I had made a wrong choice. I loved the Lord enough to register for Bible training, but this was a test of the maturity of my love. Had it matured to the level of casting out my fears?

I arrived at the college two weeks early to be sure of getting a part-time job because I had only enough money to pay for one semester, after selling my '55 Chevy. But, because I feared I might not be able to find my way back to the campus, I walked everywhere, refusing to ride a metro bus. I walked many miles, but didn't get a job until all the students arrived, because I didn't trust the bus operators enough to commit myself to them and expect them to give me proper directions to get me safely back to the dormitory. I was a victim of my fears, but worse, in my inferiority, I was too proud to admit it.

Those first nights alone in the dorm, I tried to sleep. The dormitory was an ancient two story house which had belonged to the owner of a brewery. At home in the country, there were no outdoor lights. I couldn't adjust to the streetlight beaming through the window coverings. Again and again as I drifted off to sleep, the siren of an ambulance shrieked toward a hospital a few blocks away.

WILLING AND OBEDIENT

One night after repeated attempts to get some rest, I was roused again by a siren or some creaking noise in the old house. In desperation, I cried out to God in prayer. Out of bed, I turned on the light and began reading the Bible, begging the Lord for encouragement and peace. Pastor Darrell Scott preached from Isaiah the previous Sunday, so I began reading Isaiah's first chapter. Verse nineteen arrested me: "If ye be willing and obedient, ye shall eat the good of the land."[71] I knew it was originally a promise to Israel, but I claimed it as God's promise for my situation.

God never changes. He is still eager to bless those who trust him. He strengthened me with that bit of hope from His Word. I decided to stay and try to cope with the circumstances. I remembered how God had led me to come to Omaha and decided to continue in obedience and trust. Five years later, God had given me a college degree, my sweet wife, two wonderful summers of internship under my hero among preachers, and had placed us in a church planting situation tailor-made for us. Indeed, I had eaten the good of the land! The Lord was as willing to bless me as Israel centuries before.

More recently, I attempted to witness to Mike, the most trusted prisoner on the prison compound. He worked in the Warden's office, and seemed to be respected by inmates and staff. We often conversed on other subjects, but if I tried to give him literature or address matters of faith he would hold up his hand, palm out, protesting, "Chaplain, I'm a (church affiliation)." My response was always friendly, and I respected his boundary. Occasionally he came to chapel services, Bible studies, or other events. After two years, he came forward during an invitation, declaring his newfound faith in the finished work of Christ. An intellectual of military rank, who had nearly completed a college degree in prison, he began to study the Bible and Church history with an insatiable appetite. Before long, he was bringing others to trust Christ.

SEVENTY-TWO HOUR LOCKDOWN

Mike was transferred to another prison, populated mostly with elderly convicts. Many had served long sentences, and were difficult for any outsider to reach with the gospel message. But Mike, who had served over twenty years as a prisoner, soon had a hearing among these men, conducting Bible studies and leading them to Christ.

Fog enveloped the prison, creating a security risk, because of the likelihood of attempted escape. Prisoners were locked down. The lockdown continued seventy-two hours. Just before the fog, Mike was allowed to request a cellmate of his choice. He chose an inmate who did not smoke and often read his Bible. As the lockdown began, they became acquainted. Mike soon realized the man was a cultist who didn't believe in the existence of hell, or in the deity of Christ. Using the cult's translation of the Bible, Mike first proved the existence of hell, and then began arguing for the deity of Christ. They refused meals and continued studying and debating through the night, drinking a little coffee to stay awake. During the seventy-first hour, the man dropped to his knees acknowledging Jesus Christ as his Savior, Lord, and God. Next chapel service, the new convert publicly announced to the chapel crowd that he had accepted Christ. Walking across the chapel to a waste paper receptacle, he dramatically trashed his cult version of scripture, renouncing the deception of the works-based religion.

Mike had been a believer himself just over two years! But he had garrisoned himself with the Word. He had developed his faith and learned to depend on the Father. How many church members of thirty years could use the Bible so effectively? How would you feel, locked in a cell seventy-two hours with a well-studied cultist? Jether "drew not his sword: for he feared."

BUILDING RELATIONSHIPS

Our generation has neglected the art of building relationships. We don't learn the sales clerk's name. He'll move on to another job anyway. Family relationships suffer too. Actors and entertainers are household names while we grope to recall the names of nephews or the children of our cousins. We watch people cycle through our churches and neighborhoods without ever becoming acquainted. Worse, hundreds of Bible characters are unknown to many Christians. People we work with every day are unaware that their dilemmas are begging for answers from the Word of God. These are lost opportunities to wield the sword. You are a kid only once, but you can be immature and controlled by fear all your life. You must decide.

Just as fear of the unknown grips youth, regrets and resentment paralyze the mature. Having survived a few of the storms of life, I can testify that I am no stranger to these. As I consider the tragedies of others, I cannot imagine how I would ever cope with the kinds of events they face. Then I remember that God gives his grace according to the need. Dying grace is for the dying. Since I am not dying, he hasn't yet issued any to me. In similar fashion, God infuses and enfolds His child with grace to endure divorce, murder of a loved one, rejection and misunderstanding of dear family and friends, and a thousand other trials some of us will never know. How could slaves create the beautiful enduring music of the Spirituals? They depended on their Father who gave them a measure of grace most of us cannot comprehend.

DECIDING DETERMINES THE FUTURE

"Remember now thy Creator in the days of thy youth, while the evil days come not, nor the years draw nigh, when ... they shall be afraid ... and fears shall be in the way ... " Ecclesiastes 12:1,5

Jether had no idea how vitally important that single confrontation with Zebah and Zalmunna was. To him, it was just another delay along the road home to video games and snacks. His main concern was toys and comforts of life. After all, he was "yet a youth." It's okay to be a kid. When you're a kid, others take care of you. They make the bed and clean up the bathroom. They pick up and wash clothes and replace broken glass. They pay for dry cleaning and buy new tires for your car. That's what happened. Gideon fought his son's battle for him.

Jether supposed another opportunity would come later. He would be older and wiser—better prepared. What's the hurry? Why grow up before your time? So what if Sam Walton was in business before he became a teenager? So what if Bob Jones, Sr. was preaching regularly on the Methodist circuit before he entered adolescence? My friend Bill Walker won the Omaha Youth for Christ Preacher boy contest when he was sixteen. Louis Paul Lehman was known as the boy preacher. In his seventies, he was still a Mennonite pastor with many published writings to his credit. All true enough, but everyone cannot be a child prodigy.

Looking back, it seems this was Jether's great moment. God selected this event to forever remind us that each opportunity contains the seed of destiny within it. If Jether had killed his Goliath, he could have been the next Judge of Israel. Instead, his illegitimate brother, Abimelech, eagerly usurped the position of leadership, murdered nearly the whole family, and ushered in a reign of terror, injustice, and tyranny upon the land.[72]

Jether's decision to delay decision became the fateful decision that determined his destiny. His "faith promise" would have raised deliverance for his nation and established his reputation, but instead his legacy is a single verse reiterating that he was just a kid ... just a kid. Just a kid: the double barreled excuse of an immature brat who ran with the big boys, but sucked his thumb in cowardice as his family was massacred. Jether is never again mentioned by name in the Bible. He didn't make the cut. Exit: stage left, next audition?

IS THERE A DAVID IN THE HOUSE?

Who will turn the tide in your family? Does everyone have to be consumed with envy, jealousy, and pride like Saul and Eliab, or is there a David in the house? Is an Esther waiting in the wings? Who cares that they're mocking our God? Who would notice if you choose to wait until later to decide? In some ways, every choice is a chance to decide for the future. Life keeps moving, kids!

A young man made dreadful choices that landed him in prison. I was his chaplain. We often discussed his lengthy sentence and how he could utilize the time to prepare for what will be left of his life when he walks through the sallyport to freedom. But I sadly report, he's still a kid. Often, he decided to watch television or play cards in the common area of his cell block instead of coming to Bible classes, prayer meetings, chapel services, or special evangelistic events. He is still in the clutches of the addiction that landed him in the slammer. He has a litany of excuses and lists of people to blame for his past and for the lack of state-sponsored programs he thinks should be available to help him overcome the deadly habits of fantasy thinking that control his life.

He's not so very different from hundreds of church members I've met, except the average church member is exasperated to think the prisoner can be so lackadaisical about making progress in his spiritual life. It's the old story of the log in my eye which I ignore while critiquing the speck in my friend's eye.[73]

Paul wrote some lengthy sentences in Ephesians. Everything he said was important, but if you edit some of the dependent clauses, this challenge emerges: "That we henceforth be no more children...But...may grow up."[74] Hey pal...that's it! Grow up.

MAKE A DECISION, KID

During my junior year in high school, a new plan was announced. Only those taking a test were required to be on campus during the adjusted schedule for final exams. This was a new liberty we had never enjoyed before. I took a test during the first hour followed by a two hour break. Some guys invited me to take a ride in a newly acquired car. In our town of 1,900 population, it was a big deal to "drag Main Street," cruising at fifteen to twenty miles per hour three or four blocks south, make a U turn, and retrace the route going north, make another U turn, and repeat the procedure like rats in a maze again and again. After a couple of trips up and down Central Avenue, packed three in front, three in the rear, one brilliant mind suggested that we go "to the Bluffs." The Bluffs is vernacular for the town of Scottsbluff, ten miles distant.

This was an unwelcome development for me, because it meant I could be late for my next test or miss it altogether. On top of that, I was already disobedient to my parents by merely riding with these fellows at all. But, it was inadvisable to eject from the backseat of a two door "fastback" DeSoto. So I remained silent, realizing a protest would only bring ridicule and not hasten my escape.

In Scottsbluff, the cruising procedure was repeated uneventfully. There just isn't a whole lot of excitement on a school day in January in the Bluffs. Someone said, "Let's go over to Gering." Gering is a twin city of Scottsbluff, and a quick trip across the bridge over the North Platte River. But I was worried, because we were getting farther from shore. A couple of passes through Gering, then somebody said, "Let's go to Chuck's." Chuck's is not another Nebraska panhandle town. It was a package liquor store where it was alleged that false identification was routinely accepted for underage liquor purchases.

MY DECISION TO RUN

Parked outside Chuck's rear entry, they pooled funds to buy the sauce. Nobody asked me to contribute. I was the kid who carried a Bible to school. I was certain by now that this was a set-up to get me drunk. A tall kid named Joe put on his hat, wadded the money, and pulled out his I.D. card. Joe was the outstanding actor of our school, and well known for partying and drinking exploits. He was seated directly in front of me on the passenger side next to the door. When he pulled the door latch, I shoved the seat forward and leaped onto the parking lot.

I ran like a cheetah. They pursued. One by one, they dropped out of the race until there was only one pursuer still behind me. Out of breath, I slowed to a fast walk as he caught up. "Hey, where ya going, man?"

"Not with you," I replied, looking straight ahead, avoiding eye contact.

"How ya gonna get back to school?" he panted.

"That's a big problem," I said.

He tried to convince me they would ditch the booze, and then give me a ride back. I kept walking, unconvinced that their intentions had suddenly changed.

I walked two or three miles, praying for deliverance. God provided a ride back to school in time for my exam. Next day, I learned that the guy sitting next to me in the DeSoto had barfed on the seat where I sat.

A week later, during study hall, Joe came to my desk. He dropped to one knee, looked me in the eye and said, "I respect you more than anybody I know because you wouldn't drink with us."

He said it in a whisper. No one else heard. It wasn't

announced over the intercom. But I knew I had faced the enemy and made the landmark decision. It developed my faith. I discovered my Heavenly Father would back me up in a pinch. That experience dramatically affected my future.

MISSING THE BOAT

I'm past midlife now. Some of my friends made the opposite decision. A few years ago, I was speaking and singing in a town where one of them lived. I went to visit him at his job, inviting him to come to the meeting. He had been my best friend at one time. We went to Vacation Bible School, youth retreats, and Bible camp together. He wouldn't look me in the eye. He wouldn't promise to attend nor did he tell me to "get lost." He thought he managed to delay the decision again. But he didn't. By not deciding, he chose the door marked NO.

Of all my friends, he had the most potential, graduating from high school a year ahead of schedule. He had looks, talent, personality, and leadership. He used it all to become a beer truck driver. Professional driving is an honorable job. But hauling booze is a tragic underachievement if God has created you for something better.

As we talked briefly, I looked him over. He had aged considerably. Sin does that. Teenagers in his community considered him an old geezer before he turned thirty. But he never grew up. He never matured. He missed the boat. He's still a kid. In youth, he professed Christ as his Savior, but maybe even that was a sham. Maybe he's the devil's kid. Perhaps it's not a question of growth in his case. Maybe what he really needs is to be born into the right family…God's family.

LIFE'S BIGGEST DECISION

Jesus spoke of the decision that affects our future more than any other. He compared it to a choice between a highway and a path. It's like choosing between a landscaped, well-lit Interstate and a rough mountain trail. You may be surprised that Jesus recommended the trail, not the highway. He said the broad road leads to destruction, while the narrow one leads to life.[75]

When you think about it, the main consideration in choosing a road is not the manicured rest areas or the proximity to factory outlet malls. The main question is: where does this road go? The broad road is teeming with throngs of people who have decided it is best. They have compelling arguments supporting the wisdom of their choice. Promotional advertising for the broad road is top quality, Madison Avenue variety.

The narrow path is difficult. Sometimes it is dark and difficult to see. There are many discouraging pitfalls and setbacks for these travelers. Some seem to make the trek virtually alone and with few provisions. But, Jesus pointed out that this narrow way leads to life. In another context, He said "I am the way."[76] What a narrow concept. Lots of educated people agree: that statement is too restrictive. It is an issue frequently introduced on talk shows during interviews of Christian leaders.

THE TOLERANT CHOICE

The decision to take the broad way is a choice to join most of humanity on the road that is tolerant of every idea. This philosophy says, "What is right for you may not be right for me, and vice-versa, but that's okay. Don't stress. We're all going the same way." Indeed. Everyone on this road has some kind of justification for his ideas and lifestyle. They usually point to their own good deeds to prove their way must be acceptable.

John Bunyan wrote a book about a fictitious young man who made the trip over the narrow way. In *Pilgrim's Progress*, Bunyan detailed many difficulties travelers face on the narrow path. To walk the narrow way requires casting aside one's own justifications and meritorious deeds. This path is not under the bright lights of popularity but in the eerie shadows of loneliness, rejection, and misunderstanding. This road must be walked by faith, not by sight. It requires confidence in the promises of the One who traveled it ahead of us. Jesus said of this path, "Few there be that find it."[77]

This is the decision that determines the eternal future. Where will you spend eternity? Nobody gets into Heaven on his own merit. If you think you're good enough, you're in for a shock. Only one person ever lived his life perfectly enough to earn Heaven: Jesus. He did it by never committing a single sin. If you've ever sinned once, you've already blown it. One lie! Face it: we're all sinners, except Jesus Christ.[78]

That is why the decision to receive Christ by faith is the determining choice. If Christ is in you, He will be accepted into Heaven, and you will be "accepted in the Beloved."[79] His promise is that He will never leave you nor forsake you, so when He is in you, you can't be rejected from Heaven. The Bible says it is "Christ in you, the hope of glory…"[80]

Go ahead. Decide right now. Why wait? This decision may never present itself again in your lifetime.

DECIDING YOUR FUTURE ON EARTH TOO

The decision to act in faith was ignored by Jether. Because he neglected that decision, his status and potential position in the nation Israel was tragically altered. He probably could have followed his father into a significant leadership role. Like Teddy Kennedy, his family had paved the way to his future. And, like Teddy at Chappaquiddick, one strategic decision limited forever how high he would fly.

Every opportunity to act in faith decides your future in this life and in the Kingdom of God. In several parables, Jesus taught us that our choices in this life determine our role and even our resources in His Kingdom. The Bible foretells a one thousand year reign of Christ on earth, a millennial Kingdom Age in which believers will be assigned responsibilities to rule and "reign with him."[81] Whether you interpret the Kingdom figuratively and expect its fulfillment in Heaven, or literally here on earth, scripture seems to teach that we are qualifying for future positions by how responsible we are in this life. How sad to waste the opportunities that could assure greater privilege to serve and bring glory to the Savior during his millennial reign and in Heaven's Eternal Kingdom.

WHAT ARE YOU WAITING FOR?

Now is the best time to decide. W. Clement Stone, later editor of Success Magazine, trained sales people in his insurance business, by requiring them to begin each day in a sales meeting chanting in unison "Do it now!"[82] He required them to chant "Do it now" fifty times every day. The company grew phenomenally. You cannot do everything in life. You must decide which choice is best, and do it now.

Now is the best time to decide about your personal devotional life. Now is the time to establish a family worship time. You will never get started learning how to lead others to Christ if you continue to delay. Decide! Have you neglected your wife or children? Decide now what to do about it. Are you a workaholic? Decide now to create better balance in your life. Now is the time to start a hobby, plan a mission trip, or begin supporting God's work consistently.

Is there a dream you have nurtured, imagining you will pursue it someday? Begin now to memorize scripture. Start a business now. Decide to greet everyone you meet and become the outgoing person you've wanted to be. Do you have a backlog of projects, ideas, and resources that have accumulated over the years? Decide to jettison some of them. Decide which one is the opportunity of a lifetime. Trash all the others. If you delay, you may someday realize this was the strategic moment.

Peter slept in fetters chained between two soldiers. Officers of the prison stood guard at the door. The angel of God appeared with a bright light. He slapped Peter's side, waking him, and ordered him to get up quickly. He then told Pete to fasten his belt, get on his jacket and sandals, and follow him out of the prison.[83]

That was Peter's opportunity! He could have succumbed to fear. He wasn't actually certain it was really happening. But his immediate decision to obey was the first step. As they walked through the cellblock, the locked doors opened as if automated. They kept walking, right past the guards, officers, central control, and reception officers. They were on the street in front of the prison before Pete realized it wasn't a dream! That was when he noticed the Angel had disappeared.

So, you're chained in fear. You know you're quite immature and inexperienced in the life of faith. When you hear the command, "Up and slay them!" that is the time to respond with action. One interpretation of Jether's name is that it seems to mean "overhanging."[84] I guess he was just too comfortable hanging out. After all, that is what kids do.

DECIDING IS A PROCESS

"But Daniel purposed in his heart... And Samson went down... and he turned aside to see... choose you this day..." Daniel 1:8, Judges 14:1,8, Joshua 24:15

Decision making is a process which can be broken down into component parts. Some learn the process so well in childhood that they cannot imagine the agony others endure when decision is necessary. Perhaps David was one of those fortunate people who mastered the technique early in life. His decision to challenge Goliath was no massive dilemma. But, the ease with which he made decisions became his Achilles heel when he chose Uriah's wife as his next conquest.[85]

At the other end of the spectrum is Jether, who seemed content to let others make decisions, be the heroes, and win the battles. Jether learned too late that the passive response of indecision is also a way of deciding. When the flight is on time, there is no second chance for piddle-dawdlers. The blacksmith heats the iron until it is white-hot, and he knows there is a limited window of opportunity to strike with his hammer, bending the strongest of construction materials to fabricate and accommodate his design. The chef carefully waits for the precise moment to add an ingredient that will make his dish delectable. Life is full of illustrations of the strategic moment and of the tragedy of its loss.

IT IS A SCIENCE

Decision making is scientific. Military training eliminates as many decisions as possible by inculcating conditioned responses to specific policy-driven choices. Jether's inability to decide seems out of character for a trained soldier. But, many a Christian struggles with making and adhering to policy decisions about devotional reading, meditation, prayer, and witnessing. The discipline of a daily and weekly schedule pays great dividends over the long haul. Scripture knowledge is not mastered by crash courses, revivals, and seminars, but by daily exposure to "precept upon precept, precept upon precept; line upon line, line upon line; here a little, and there a little … "[86]

The ability to witness and present the gospel competently to many different kinds of individuals is more caught than taught, being the result of familiarity with the information and how people process it, along with development of receptivity to the "still small voice" of the Holy Spirit. There is no better way to adopt conditioned responses for decision making in witnessing than by regular forays into "enemy territory" in "war games" or better yet, in actual engagements on the street or in homes. In the arena is where decisiveness is developed for any skill, whether driving a vehicle or operating a mixing board in an audio production studio.

Anything can be done better systematically than by haphazard chance. Eliminating loss is as necessary to success in business as is the predictability of a profit margin. Policies provide ready-made decisions that save time and energy. Policy driven decision making is built on the foundation of careful observation, analysis, modification, and testing.

Before electricity and automated heating and air conditioning, people went to bed shortly after sundown and arose at dawn. Changing this habit was not a snap decision. Many were resistant to change. Decades after the flexibility provided by electric lights, people still resist Daylight Savings Time. We must examine why we resist new policy. Why do you put off making a policy that will govern future decisions? Why reject established practices or resist new ones? The science of decision begins with such questions.

YOU CAN MASTER THE SKILL

Olan Hendrix taught Christian workers that management skills can be learned.[87] As the science of leadership spun off from management philosophy, John Maxwell and others distilled principles of leadership, emphasizing that most of us can improve leadership skill.[88] Deciding is just one of the skills leaders and managers must master.

For decades, many supposed sales technique was raw talent. One was either born with or without a bent for selling. An innovative wave of thoughtful marketers championed the new model of selling[89] to a generation that learned more could be accomplished by a scientific approach to sales as consulting rather than arm-twisting.

As in the mastery of any skill, one must focus attention on the components of the process, eliminate bad habits that hinder it, create or adopt a model—an agenda to follow, refine, and upgrade the model through a process of analysis and frequent review, and then practice, practice, practice.

Unlike military training, this conditioning is rarely done in a culture dish environment. Therefore, the recruit must recognize that mastery of decision making skill may meet with resistance from others who expect relationships to remain the same. If you have been known to be passive, acquiescing to others' decisions, your initial attempts at change will probably meet with resistance, if not outright ridicule. Mental preparation similar to an athlete's attitude cultivation will be essential. You may need to have a talk with family and friends to enlist a support group who will encourage you and keep you accountable for progress. No pain... no gain.

A radical change of environment may enable change. As a seventeen year old teen, I enrolled in a college far from home where virtually nobody knew me as the bashful, backward country boy. I had attempted to change my outlook and social habits during high school by forcing myself to be outgoing at my job in a supermarket. Minimal success there and encouragement from Pastor Larry Carrier, who gave me a booklet on developing self-confidence,[90] sparked hope that major change was possible. The only people at the college with whom I had any prior relationship were mere acquaintances, though one, Dennis Gingrich, was to become my close friend for several years. Had it not been for the encouragement of these, I might have given up on change, like I gave up on playing piano and trombone.

Though I failed miserably in my one opportunity to solo with my high school choir, I aggressively pursued tryouts for the select Chorale and scholarship quartet in college. There were more set-backs, but the initial trauma of change wasn't so bad after all. Ultimately, the radical change worked for me, because I was determined to take advantage of the opportunity.

PERMANENCE NOT GUARANTEED

It is only fair to disclose my struggle with relapses. At critical times, I have retreated into my shell because I entertained thoughts of defeat, which eventually got the upper hand for a time. After some twenty years of successes, pride whispered that my victory was permanent. Then, through tests of strategic resistance to my leadership combined with increased vulnerability due to economic stress and unexpected responsibility with the illness of my aging parents, I faltered.

A major project in our ministry was the opening of a new Christian radio station. At the crucial moment, our promised satellite provider pulled the plug, discontinuing service. Trends in our oil and mineral recovery based economy caused massive loss of employment and scores of families moved out of our region. Financial reversals steadily took their toll. I began to second-guess decisions, blame, and make excuses. This led to an untimely move to another state. The radio station discontinued operation a few months later.

I tried to bluff my way through new problems, while steadily losing confidence and abandoning personal disciplines. Several snap decisions proved harmful. More than eight years later, I accepted defeat and withdrew, enlisting in a prison ministry halfway across the country. With insufficient financial support and a new constituency unfamiliar with my earlier successes, I found myself plunging deeper into self recrimination and depression.

As I look back, I see a steady trend away from the disciplined decision-making practices that I had learned during my initial career building era. During the crash and burn stage of my life, an offhand remark made by one of my associates was, "Anyone who cannot make a decision ought to get out of leadership." He was right. I do not know whether he meant to address the comment to me, but like a heat-seeking missile, it found its mark.

Just as the Apostle Peter experienced major relapses, no one is guaranteed permanent success. It must be defended, maintained and reclaimed. Some of us find ourselves singing "Revive us again" more frequently than we wish. Peter arrogantly asserted his loyalty to Christ, but Jesus knew him better than he knew himself. Jesus predicted that he would deny him and be disloyal within twenty-four hours. When Peter realized how low he had gone, he went out and wept bitterly. Even after Jesus rose from the dead and sent a special personalized message to Peter, the disillusioned disciple made another self-destructive decision. He decided to go back to fishing, leaving his calling. That choice influenced most of the disciples to bail out with him.[91] Jesus never criticized or condemned him. He showed up along the shore and invited Peter to breakfast! What an amazing Lord and leader he is.

After Peter was greatly used of God to preach on the day of Pentecost, and later to begin outreach to Gentiles, he decided to withdraw, refusing to associate with Gentile converts because it would be unpopular with Jewish believers. Paul rebuked him face to face.[92] Peter got back on track and went on to have a tremendous ministry, writing two books of the New Testament, and eventually making the ultimate sacrifice, being martyred by crucifixion.

Have you made some bad decisions? Make some good ones. Get back on the path to blessing.

SNAP DECISIONS CAN BE RIGHT

The shoot-from-the-hip decision is desirable and may be absolutely essential at times. Snap decisions are familiar territory to the basketball player or the football captain. No less should they be the domain of a Christian. Many a prime opportunity is lost by those who deliberate, because they have not thoughtfully trained for the crucial moment. Jether's delay seems to shout "Lack of Preparation" or at least "Lack of Discipline." Daniel purposed in his heart well in advance of the crisis, which qualified him to choose his course of action with ease, confidence, and without a glance toward the alternative.[93]

The movie, Chariots of Fire[94] immortalized the decisive choice of Eric Liddell, who had long before established a boundary which he refused to violate. Nearly a century later, the world still pauses for reflection and gazes longingly, perplexed at the conviction of an athlete who refused to compete on Sunday. Some think him a fool, but eternity will tell.

TAKE TIME IF YOU CAN

Times of fasting and extended periods of prayer were a regular part of our Lord's regimen. Extensive consideration of circumstances, funding, logistics, and one's own motives may be the only strategy which will help sort out alternatives and evaluate potential consequences. Daniel's twenty-one day fast with prayer yielded amazing spiritual insight, including prophetic vision and understanding of scripture.[95] People demand sudden commitments, but discernment may dictate delay. Dr. Lee Roberson was well known for his method of teaching this concept to those who came to him for counsel. Taking a pen, he would draw a large question mark on a 3x5 card. Handing it to the counselee, he said, "Don't move until God removes this."

By adopting guiding principles and sticking to them, many decisions can be settled well in advance. Unfortunately, the discipline required to maintain such standards of conduct ignores the danger in smug neglect of similar disciplines in the hidden life of prayer and devotion. Samson might have avoided many temptations, torture, and even his untimely death if he had consistently honored principles of the heart as religiously as he followed the external demands of his Nazarite vow. As a teen and later as an evangelist to teens, my focus was too often upon the adoption of standards of conduct with little emphasis on matters of the inner devotional life. While carefully guarding myself against "worldly amusements and questionable practices" in an effort to maintain a reputation worthy of my calling, I gradually permitted secret ambitions to blossom with pride, which is perhaps the most destructive allurement offered by Satan. In my recovery from the crisis, I learned that loneliness of private times of fasting and prayer are more than compensated by the companionship and confidence obtained from the indwelling Spirit and abiding Christ.

DON'T AGONIZE

When indecision continues beyond reasonable limitations, a deadline must be set. The choice must be prayerfully executed by the deadline. Some personalities agonize interminably unless forced to choose. If you know yourself to be continually caught in the doldrums of indecision, a deadline combined with accountability to a trusted friend may be the only way to break the habit of procrastination in crucial decisions.

MAKE IT A HABIT

Leaders know that someone must seize the moment. Quarterbacks must decide, and those who draw back repeatedly find themselves on the bench. Habitual decisiveness, taking the lead before others do so, attracts followers and accomplishes prescribed goals. Adrian House developed the habit of setting the pace and played varsity high school football when he was only an eighth grader. After a short stint on an automaker's assembly line, he joined the Marine Corps. His compelling leadership was stifled on the assembly line. Following service in Korea, he enrolled in BIOLA College, ascended to the office of Student Body President, graduated, completed seminary, directed a Bible camp in Colorado, served as pastor in a small Nebraska town, and founded a new church in Wyoming's capitol city. BIOLA invited him back as Alumni Director, and he was soon recruited to the Presidency of Western Bible College. Within five years, the student body doubled, finances moved from a deficit into the black, new buildings including a student union, married student apartments, and a President's Home were completed, and radio station KWBI-FM grew from a four hour per day operation to a growing network reaching Colorado and beyond. He was selected over men with more advanced academic degrees and years of experience in education, because he was inspiringly decisive. Every organization he led benefited from his well developed habit of deciding.

ERRORS OF JETHER'S FATAL DECISION

"Pride hath budded… and thou shalt no more be haughty… Pride goeth before destruction, and an haughty spirit before a fall." Ezekiel 7:10, Zephaniah 3:11, Proverbs 16:18

Often, a person congratulates himself on making a successful choice, and relaxes, savoring the moment. Jether may have been quite impressed with himself for having achieved the status he enjoyed in the military chain of command. The temptation to rest on his laurels would not be uncommon among youth. At age thirty-three, Alexander the Great wept that there were no more worlds to conquer and overlooked the greatest challenge of all: the battle to conquer self. Nebuchadnezzar, caught up in admiring his achievements, failed to see the arrogance within that jettisoned him into seven years of insanity.[96] Major accomplishments early in life often become barriers to greater vistas.

HE FORGOT THAT LIFE KEEPS MOVING

Many prisoners are immobilized by regret. They suppose that the tragic decision to commit a crime destroyed everything in their future. One boy went to prison as a juvenile. He grew up watching his step-grandfather habitually molest and abuse children of the family. One day while sexually harassing a younger sister, the abuser pulled off his western style belt, threatening to whip her with the buckle. Her brother bolted into another room and returned with a firearm. Firing at close range, he murdered the molester. He will be nearly sixty years of age before his time is served. The snap decision that sealed his fate robbed him of the confidence to make a decision and stick to it. He drifts from one religious group to another unable to decide whether he should be a Muslim, Wiccan, Jehovah's Witness, Catholic, Methodist or Baptist.

Contrast the way Joseph utilized his experience in slavery and prison to keep growing, ever trusting God to fulfill the dreams of his childhood. Life keeps moving, but some get stuck in resentment, regret, bitterness, and indecision. Whatever stymied Jether when he faced the enemy had more to do with his past than it did with his future. How sad that he never figured it out.

ASSUMING HE'D ALREADY MADE THE WATERSHED DECISION

One older Christian laments the poor choices of his youth. Challenged to launch out by faith, his customary reply is, "It's too late for me. The bird with the broken pinion never flew so high again." Supposing that you've already made the ultimate decision will stifle creativity, smother imagination, and blindfold you, blocking the path of faith and short-circuiting confidence in the God of miracles. Think of all the miracles God brought into Moses' life when he turned his attention from the fatal choice that labeled him a murderer:

ten plagues upon Egypt, a rod that doubled as a live snake, the opening of the Red Sea, destruction of Pharaoh's army, water from the Rock, manna in the wilderness, a miracle cure for snakebite, and many more.

Ahithophel, known for his erudite counsel, became obsessed with another man's wrong. David had seduced the old counselor's granddaughter and ordered the execution of her husband, Uriah. With unparalleled arrogance, he aggravated the injury when he married the beautiful granddaughter, Bathsheba. Reacting, Ahithophel devoted all his energy and influence to support David's political opponent, the godless Absolom. Surely he knew better. But, when his advice to Absolom was ignored, he anticipated the worst outcome and in an impetuous moment, committed suicide.[97] How could he abandon the wisdom of a lifetime and deny his alienated friend an opportunity for reconciliation? Will we someday learn how God wanted to turn the curse into a blessing and give Ahithophel an unprecedented privilege to reflect the grace and mercy of his Redeemer by extending the same to David? But he, like Jether, assumed he had already made his final choice.

UNWILLING TO RISK

Esau was so angry about Jacob's treacherous manipulations that he declared his plan for revenge and promised to kill his own twin.[98] What if he had rejoiced in the good fortune of his brother instead? History might have told a different story of diplomatic relations between Israel and the Edomites, Esau's descendents. Though the twins finally buried the hatchet,[99] bitter hatred remained in the hearts of their children. The Old Testament prophet Obadiah described the bloody final chapter of the Edomites, who held a grudge for hundreds of years. When we neglect to repair relationships, the poison spreads to family and friends, who may never recover.

Jether's family relationships with so many stepmothers and their kids (at least seventy sons of Gideon) had to be difficult, influencing his choices. Choices affect attitudes, which in turn continue to impact other decisions. His relationship to his father must have brought him to decide to be reserved, remaining withdrawn, not risking too much.

THE ALLURE OF PEACEFUL COEXISTENCE

"Up and slay them," was Gideon's command. The old warrior knew that it will never do to peacefully coexist with the enemy. Soft modern Christians think they have no sworn enemies of significance.[100] Satan's invisible host is out of sight, out of mind. Slaying enemies of the spirit world is for many an inconvenient consideration among priorities of the fast paced lives we live. The New Testament way is, "mortify the deeds of the body."[101] Too late, when his half brother murdered their entire family (except one brother, Jotham), Jether learned his enemies were bent on destruction.[102] Free world Christians enjoy liberties purchased by our ancestors, but lurking in the shadows, enemies of the cross of Christ plot mayhem and massacre. Hitler and Stalin's brands of totalitarianism still inspire misguided youth around the world who will yet rise up hoping to establish the futile Marxist deception. While believers leisurely ride in the parade singing "Onward Christian Soldiers", masses of Christ-hating socialists, religionists, and humanists attack Christmas celebrations and Biblical displays, ever pushing toward their declared goal of eliminating the "intolerant" Christian faith from earth's domain. Shall we take an aggressive stance, or tolerate their insidious demands? Who will draw the sword?

Of greater consequence, bad habits, cursing, rebellion against parents, sinful covetousness and indulgent lusts are all dressed up in acceptable attire. Peacefully, we coexist with those who take God's name in vain, cheat, steal, lie, and rob by practices protected by law and reinforced by the precedents of decadent courts, movie makers, and media pacesetters. Peacefully, we coexist with those who dumb down our Sunday schools, and vote by absence to discontinue regular services of the church while children and young believers plunge ignorantly on, oblivious of how little Scripture they really understand. Too late, they awake to the loss of their children, whose concept of Christianity is an affront to those who were burned at the stake for merely naming the name of Christ.

CHASING BUBBLES

Flippant decisions are exit ramps to delayed choices that stretch out like endless detours. Mark and Torrey House were just toddlers when I watched them blow bubbles in the back yard. Mark dipped the wand into the soapy liquid and blew bubbles galore. Growing impatient, Torrey the younger one, amused himself chasing bubble after bubble, grabbing and giggling with delight. Mark, increasingly frustrated, tried to guard the bubbles from their inevitable extinction. Adults and teens mirror the exercise, either chasing bubbles that burst, only to launch out on an excursion for yet another bubble or vainly protecting their dream bubbles, which can never satisfy the craving the shiny bubbles promise to fulfill.

Unworthy goals and small ambitions consume whole lives like boa constrictors swallowing their prey. Obsessed with Guiness World Record fame as a peanut pusher, one fellow rigged a wire contraption mounted on his head with a projection designed to shove a peanut forward as he proceeded on all fours up the steep incline of Pike's Peak.[103] The record, I'm told, shows the exact number of peanut shells worn out on the journey, along with the distance crawled and elapsed time.

Nothing is preserved to inform us of the unworthy ambitions that distracted Jether. But human nature everywhere demonstrates that mankind always focuses on some kind of peanut rolling or bubble chasing. Perhaps Jether was an expert on different models and styles of swords, rattling off the names and scores of swordsmen in the Annual Israeli swordfights. Maybe his dream was to restore an ancient fencing center. He might as well have pushed peanuts up Mt. Carmel or chased bubbles at the Feast of Tabernacles.

Bubble chasing may serve some recreational value. Everyone needs some form of stress dissipation. But, what if Charles Spurgeon had nurtured a bubble obsession? Imagine John Bunyan consumed with a legacy of peanut pushing instead of the progress of a pilgrim? Jerry Falwell and James Kennedy pursued goals as worthy as those of Benjamin Franklin or George Whitefield while peanut pushing critics chased bubbles of pleasure or ground axes of personal preference they could have wielded against the idols of late twentieth century American church goers.

But...What is your decision? What bubble has distracted you from the real battle? How many more peanuts will eject from worn out shells before you decide to devote your zeal to the worthy cause planted in your heart by the God of Destiny and nurtured by the prayers of greater souls who envisioned your success and dedicated their precious energy to the hope that you would rise to the occasion? Can you hear our Captain? Up, and slay them!

ENDNOTES

1. II Timothy 2:3
2. http://encyclopedia.jrank.org/CLI_COM/COLERIDGE_HARTLEY_1796_1849_.html
3. Judges 8:20
4. I Chronicles 4:9–10
5. Judges 8: 13–21
6. Judges 8:20
7. (Copeland, c.1973)
8. Judges 8: 30–31
9. Judges 9:5
10. Colossians 3:21
11. Exodus 20:5
12. Judges 8:21
13. (Tracy, 1987)
14. (Ward, 1888) p.72.
15. Ibid.
16. Romans 12:3
17. Romans 10:17
18. Psalm 84:7
19. Romans 1:17
20. Ephesians 6: 17

21	Hebrews 4:12
22	I Samuel 17:45
23	Hebrews 4:12
24	Acts 4:13
25	Ephesians 5:18
26	Judges 13:25
27	Job 32:8
28	Acts 6:5
29	Isaiah 28:10
30	(Glover, 1959)
31	(Clark, 1975)
32	Joel 3:14
33	(Terry, 1972) p. 129.
34	Ibid p. 135.
35	Judges 6:37–40
36	Proverbs 16:18
37	(Douglas, 1966) p. 29.
38	II Samuel 12:7
39	Psalm 51:17
40	(Tenney, 1963); and (Strong, 1963)
41	Revelation 3:17
42	Joshua 24:15
43	Isaiah 28:10
44	Romans 10:17
45	Judges 6:25–27
46	Matthew 6:33
47	Joshua 7:1–11
48	I Kings 10:23

49	I Kings 12:16
50	Proverbs 26:16
51	Proverbs 26:12
52	Judges 8:18
53	John 1:11–12
54	John 8:44
55	Genesis 19:16
56	(Waitley, 1986) p. 240.
57	(LaHaye, 1993) p. 103.
58	Acts 5:29
59	(Dallimore, 1979)
60	Ibid p. 116, 296, 438–9, 441, 481–2, Vol. II, p. 222, 223, 440–53.
61	I John 4:18, II Timothy 1:7
62	Genesis 3:10
63	I John 1:9
64	Luke 12:32
65	Hebrews 13:5–6
66	John 1:12
67	Romans 10:9–10
68	Genesis 22:1–19
69	I John 2:5
70	(Vine, 1966)
71	Isaiah 1:19
72	Judges 9:5, cf. 6:32
73	Matthew 7:3–5
74	Ephesians 4:14–15
75	Matthew 7:13–14

76	John 14:6
77	Matthew 7:14
78	Romans 3:23, Hebrews 4:15
79	Ephesians 1:6
80	Hebrews 13:5, Colossians 1:27
81	Revelation 20:4,6
82	(Tracy, 1988) p. 168.
83	Acts 12:3–11
84	Op. Cit., (Strong, 1987) p. 53, # 3499, 3500
85	II Samuel 11:2
86	Isaiah 28:10
87	(Hendrix, 1975)
88	(Maxwell, 1998)
89	Op. Cit., (Tracy, 1987)
90	(Narramore, 1963)
91	John 21:3–13
92	Galatians 2:11–14
93	Daniel 1:8
94	(Welland, 1981)
95	Daniel 10:2–13
96	Daniel 4:30–37
97	II Samuel 16:23, 17:23
98	Genesis 27:41
99	Genesis 33:4, Obadiah 1:6–15
100	Revelation 3:17
101	Romans 8:13, Colossians 3:5
102	Judges 9:5
103	Reported to the author by a National Park ranger who worked on Pikes Peak, 1972.

BIBLIOGRAPHY

Clark, E. Nothing is Impossible. *Songs You Love.* Good News Broadcasting Association, Inc., Lincoln, NE, USA.

Dallimore, A. (1979). *George Whitefield* (Vol. I). Westchester, IL: Cornerstone Books.

Douglas, M. (1966). *How to Make a Habit of Succeeding.* Grand Rapids, MI: Zondervan.

Glover, A. (1959). *A Thousand Miles of Miracle in China.* Chicago, IL: Moody Press.

Hendrix, O. (1975). *Olan Hendrix Management Skills Seminar.* Philadelphia: Olan Hendrix.

LaHaye, T. F. (1993). *Spirit Controlled Temperment.* Wheaton, IL: Tyndale House Publishers.

Maxwell, J. C. (1998). *The 21 Irrefutable Laws of Leadership.* Nashville, TN: Thomas Nelson.

Moyers, B. (c.1973). Quotable Quotes. *Reader's Digest* .

Narramore, Clyde M. (1963). *Improving Your Self-Confidence.* Grand Rapids: Zondervan.

Strong, J. (1963). *A Concise Dictionary of the Hebrew Bible.* New York: Abingdon Press.

Tenney, M. C. (Ed.). (1963). *Zondervan Pictorial Bible Dictionary.* Grand Rapids, MI: Zondervan.

Terry, G. R. (1972). *Principles of Management.* Homewood, IL: Richard D. Irwin, Inc.

Tracy, B. (1987). *The New Psychology of Selling.* San Diego: Brian Tracy Learning Systems.

Tracy, B. (1988). *The Phoenix Seminar.* San Diego: Brian Tracy Learning Systems.

Vine, W. (1966). *Expository Dictionary of New Testament Words.* Westwood: Fleming H. Revell.

Welland, C. (1981). *Chariots of Fire* . (H. Hudson, Director, B. Cross, Performer) New York.

Waitley, D. &. Tucker, W. (1986). *Winning the Innovation Game.* Old Tappan: Fleming H. Revell.

Ward, J. H. (Ed.). (1888). *Cyclopedia of Practical Quotations.* New York, NY: Funk & Wagnalls.

listen|imagine|view|experience

AUDIO BOOK DOWNLOAD INCLUDED WITH THIS BOOK!

In your hands you hold a complete digital entertainment package. Besides purchasing the paper version of this book, this book includes a free download of the audio version of this book. Simply use the code listed below when visiting our website. Once downloaded to your computer, you can listen to the book through your computer's speakers, burn it to an audio CD or save the file to your portable music device (such as Apple's popular iPod) and listen on the go!

How to get your free audio book digital download:

1. Visit www.tatepublishing.com and click on the e|LIVE logo on the home page.
2. Enter the following coupon code:
   d806-fd2b-7c47-aad7-25cd-e10f-5dbd-ca59
3. Download the audio book from your e|LIVE digital locker and begin enjoying your new digital entertainment package today!